NATURE VS. MAN

NATURE VS. MAN

About socialist ideals foreign to Nature:
Enforced Equality (live as others)
Coerced Altruism (live for others) and
Suppressed Human Nature (think like others)

By
Valdemar Malin

Nature vs. Man

Published in the United States by Booklocker.com, Inc., Bangor, Maine. Printed in the United States of America on acid-free paper.

Booklocker.com, Inc.
2012

Second Edition

To my precious grand-daughter and daughter with concern and hope for their future.

To my beloved wife who filled my life with life, love and joy.

And to my dear late parents who gave me everything they had.

ABOUT THE AUTHOR

Dr. Valdemar Malin, an internationally recognized engineer and scientist, was born in the former USSR. He spent the first half of his life living behind the Iron Curtain, until he immigrated to the US in 1979. Since then, he worked for the U.S. Government, in private industry and academia. During his distinguished career in the US, Dr. Malin has published more than 50 scientific articles and books and has received numerous national and international awards for his advanced research and technological innovations. Dr. Malin is a Fellow of the American Welding Society.

From kindergarten through his college graduation, Dr. Malin was brainwashed to believe that socialism was the road to the Promised Land, a utopia of equality, and a society of willing altruists living in freedom and devoid of natural human vices.

However, the grim reality contradicted all he was taught about socialism. Dr. Malin discovered first-hand that socialism did not bring equality, prosperity or freedom. On the contrary, the only equality it generated was an equal share of poverty, scarcity, despair and misery for everyone except for the ruling class.

Having spent decades working in socialist industry, he became familiar also with the incredible inefficiency and waste of resources; across-the-board pilfering of government-owned property; the absence of incentives, corruption and the overall employee apathy—the results of the total absurdity of the artificially created, unnatural socialist economic system.

Dr. Malin wrote this book as an eye-witness account about this system and its hidden agenda—the system that defies Nature and human nature. And he didn't do it alone but in cooperation with the ultimate authority on the subject … Her

Majesty Nature, the epitome of wisdom, respect and credibility. He let Nature do the talking in clear, simple, "natural" language mixed with convincing visuals rather than boring statistics.

Now, you have a chance to listen to what Nature has to say about the socio-economic system that has failed in every place across the world where it has been tried; the system that is rising here, in the US—the very last place on Earth to escape its grip.

TABLE OF CONTENT

PROLOGUE

...A man found a cocoon. A helpless butterfly is struggling desperately inside of it. It is not able to get out through a narrow hole. The man opens up the cocoon with a knife and lets the butterfly out. But what a disappointment! Instead of a butterfly, a sick creature emerges from the cocoon dragging its feeble, shivering body and unable to spread its wings for the rest of its life.

This is an anonymous fable called "The Story of the Butterfly" I found browsing the Internet one day. It drew my attention instantly because it was about Nature, Man and Life. The powerful conclusions of the story were both moralistic and motivational. Man asks Life to give him strength, but receives difficulties to overcome. Man asks for wisdom, but is slapped with problems to solve. Man asks for wealth, but gets brain and muscles to work hard. Man does not get everything he asks, but Life gave Man everything he needs to succeed.

What a beautiful and uplifting story! It exposes Man's petty grievances to wise and caring Nature. Still, something bothered me about the story; something was hidden, missing or overlooked. Only later, it occurred to me what it was—the story was, in fact, about Nature's grievances to undeserving Man— profound, philosophical grievances although invisible for a naked eye.

Why did Man let the butterfly out, in the first place? Why did Man interfere with Nature? It was because he saw other butterflies hatched successfully—healthy and ready to fly! And here come the feelings of compassion and injustice, as well as altruistic desire: "Oh, the poor thing needs help! The hole is too small, huh! It's not fair!" And Man helped. He feels good, wise and righteous—he freed a disadvantaged butterfly, after all.

But did Man do the right thing in the eyes of Nature? Absolutely not! Nature cares about the results, not intentions. In the eyes of Nature, what Man did is a cruel, ignorant and wrong act; it is a flagrant violation of the rules of Life.

Just look around and think what Nature does—Nature gives equal opportunities to all butterflies but does not guarantee success. But Man wants the guarantees and equal results. Man gave a "less fortunate" butterfly *a free ride*...and the poor thing came out underdeveloped, crippled and condemned to a dreadful existence for life.

Nature makes an opening in a cocoon intentionally small so that a butterfly stays inside and works hard until it develops its wings; but Man's ignorance let it free too early. A butterfly has to earn its wings—give it *a free lunch*...and it will never fly.

Nature's intention is to preserve life of a butterfly; Man's— to fix "errors" of Nature. With a knife of good intentions, misguided compassion and blind *altruism,* Man ruined Life.

...That's exactly what is wrong with socialism: Man interferes with Nature and defies the rules of Life. And Nature condemns a socialist society to be underdeveloped, crippled and doomed to failure.

...And this is what this book is all about. I called it Nature vs. Man as depicted allegorically on the cover. Here, Man, a little, pitiful living being, sticks its finger right into the face of Almighty Nature. And Nature does not take it lightly—Man is moving blindly toward and is already one step from the abyss.

This book is not a research study, a science fiction, a novel or a satire. It is an open conversation between Nature and anyone who wants to listen. You may call it a fantasy and walk away at your peril; or you can stop for a moment and listen too.

This book is about Nature, Man and Life; about strained relationships between arrogant Man and tolerant Nature; about Man's delusions of being wiser than, superior to and above

Nature; and about stunning, incomprehensible miracles of Life created by Nature.

This book is not about Nature's beauty—it is about Nature's wisdom. It is about Nature's genius inventions Man discovers every day in astonishment and admiration, which dwarf everything Man has ever achieved.

This book is about the eternal rules of Life created by Nature that never failed to benefit all living things, including Man. These rules pursue the ultimate goal—PRESERVATION OF LIFE and they are familiar to and followed by every living thing on the planet Earth:

Life is about equal Opportunity—not Equality.
Free ride and free lunch ruin Life and contradict Nature.
Competition and incentives are the driving force of Life.
Life is about working hard to earn one's keep.
Life is about keeping and protecting what one earns.
Self-interest is the way of Life—altruism defies Nature.

So, why does Man ignore these rules of Life? Why does Man consider them primitive, erroneous and outright wrong? Why, in the world, Man does not want to learn from, but wants to get rid of these rules of Nature? There is the only one plausible, but frightening explanation—*Man does not care about preservation of Life as Nature does!*

This book is about life-faking fantasies called socialism, which is born in a limited human mind; rejects rules of Life; fails to benefit Man; defies Nature and human nature. I didn't write this book alone; I've got help from the ultimate authority on the subject...Her Majesty Nature—the epitome of wisdom, respect and credibility. I let Nature do the talking in clear, simple "natural" language mixed with convincing visuals rather than boring statistics.

This is an eye-witness account about socialism, its ideals and its hidden agenda. I came to the US from a socialist country formerly called USSR. Everything in that country was against Nature and offensive to human nature. We were forced to march in steps as one collective body singing in unison only one song: "I don't know any other country where Man is breathing so freely!"

But what a lie it was! The USSR was not a country; it was a strange planet Nature has never seen before. It was an alien world, isolated and hermetically sealed. No one was breathing freely there—there was no oxygen on that planet! Those who conformed received a respirator and a rationed dose of oxygen to breathe. The rest were cut off from the oxygen supply.

Opposite to Nature, everything on that planet was according to their socio-economic theories—upside down. Poverty was considered prosperity; life in hard-labor camps was called freedom; the brave were put away—the cowards were saluted; the achievers were punished—the losers were rewarded; the honest were despised and demoted—the corrupted were held in high esteem and promoted.

They told us to walk upside down, and we obeyed them. They assured us that it was not natural to walk upright, and we believed them. They ordered us to keep our heads down, and we did not dare to look up over the horizon.

But I did dare to look over the horizon one day, and I have seen people there walking upright with their heads up and without respirators. To my horror, I realized that I was walking the wrong way up all my life. I did not believe them anymore, and I did not want to keep my head down ever again.

I left behind that perverted world, the only world I have ever known, risking my life. I came to a new world where people lived by strange principles of free-market capitalism; self-interest and self-reliance they taught me to hate.

I fell in love with this new world and its people, for life. I fell in love with the powerful ideals of their founding fathers; the principles by which this great country lives, among them— *Life, Liberty and Pursuit of happiness.* These ideals have turned this country into the envy of the world. I came here to give my daughter a chance to live by these principles too.

Bad dreams! Something happened in recent years, and I cannot recognize this country any more. These ideals have been trampled and are under increasing attacks. *New progressive, socialist, collectivist* ideals are creeping everywhere. They are in disguise covering their faces under ski masks, but I recognize them. To my horror, they are the same painfully familiar ideals I lived by in the country I used to call my home. They are the same "progressive" ideals worshipped by all socialists and the most fundamental ones pursue the ultimate goals:

To force economic equality (live as others),

To coerce altruism (live for others) and

To suppress human nature (think like others).

These socialist ideals come together as one package. Since *equality* means taking from others, it cannot be achieved without a tool called *"live-for-others" altruism*; since equality and altruism go against *human nature*, the latter should be suppressed and "rejuvenated." These socialist ideals go against Nature because Man does not understand Nature's intentions. They are foreign to human nature as well, and they are drenched in blood of millions sacrificed human lives.

I thought that these bankrupted socialist ideals had gone in flames after the catastrophic failure of communism around the world. I thought that the ideals of free-market capitalism had prevailed—the ideals based on competition, private property rights, self-interest and freedom to do what you like at your own risk. Nature created, endorsed and sponsored these principles—not a little human mind.

I was wrong! Unnatural ideas born in a human mind do not go away by themselves. Like deadly germs in Nature, they come back if you do not fight them off every minute, every day with everything you've got. Obviously, we did not! Here, they are crawling again stealthily ruining this beautiful country; hiding behind noble causes of economic equality; masquerading as altruistic actions of helping the poor; and misrepresenting the true human nature.

It is so ironic today that the socialists with and without ski masks are asking you for the second chance. They say that the socialist ideals were not wrong—the people who implemented them were wrong. Oh, come on, socialists! For decades, you kept saying that socialism in the USSR was the envy of the entire world; that it was a perfect model for the humanity; that it carried the torch and led the way into the future. Now, you are saying that socialism in the USSR was not real socialism; that you are not trying to build socialism here in the US!

And many of us do believe them that our country is not moving toward socialism, one legislative act at a time. Really! Just imagine that socialism is a tree—roots, branches and leaves. The socialist ideals (economic equality or live-for-others altruism) are the roots—the foundation of the tree that supplies nutrients (legislative acts) to the leaves. But the roots are usually hidden deep underground.

This book traces those legislative acts to the roots; it unearths the roots and exposes them to the sun light! It exposes progressive, socialist ideals rising from their graves and walking into our life like the living dead.

And here is my final point. On the Nature's scale of time, Man is an infant and therefore, knows very little about Nature and has limited abilities to comprehend Nature's intentions. On the Nature's scale of things, Man's achievements are primitive in comparison with the eternal and incomprehensible world ingeniously created by Nature. Man is just scratching the surface of this world.

To their demise, the socialist ideals prescribe the way Man has to live in this world as a society, but they do not borrow their ideas from Nature, and therefore, are artificial, impractical and unsustainable. They are claimed to be based on principles superior to anything offered by Nature, but they are created by a limited human mind, and therefore, are as primitive as everything else created by Man. Their good intentions are to correct "mistakes" made by Nature to the benefits of humanity, but they reject the eternal, time-proven and flawless rules of Life, and therefore, are incurably wrong, destructive to humanity and doomed to failure.

Nature takes these socialist ideals to court—not to the Court of LAW (as we do too often), but to … the Court of NATURE! Here, they are subjected to merciless scrutiny of the presiding Honorable Judge...Almighty Nature. YOU are summoned to serve as a juror in this court. You can serve or excuse yourself. Just remember, the wrong verdict will affect your life and your children's lives profoundly and irreversibly.

I am not a public defender in this court—Nature does not need one, but Nature needs a friend. This book is a call from a friend, a desperate wake up call.

Chapter 1
WISDOM: NATURE VS. MAN

IS WISDOM OF MAN SUPERIOR TO WISDOM OF NATURE?

Bella Plays a Puzzle-Game

One hot summer, my wife and I came to New Jersey from Chicago to visit our daughter. We came to baby sit our granddaughter, while her mom and dad went on vacation abroad.

Almost 4-year old, Isabella is a pretty smart and playful little kitten. I am sitting on the floor in her bedroom upstairs watching her as she plays a puzzle-game. She needs to put in place a bunch of cards together. Each card is of irregular shape with small lips and cutouts for engagement with other matching cards around it. When all the cards are locked in place correctly, a beautiful landscape appears before your eyes. A white castle on the top of distant hills is sparkling in the sun; a beautiful river is crawling down from those hills like a dark-blue snake. Green water meadows and young tree groves are stretching far away on both banks of the river under the blue, bright sky.

Each time Bella locks in place the right card, we both cheer loudly and applaud as if she made a new, important discovery. We played this game before and had a lot of fun. But this time, it was different.

"Bella, this card does not match; take another one," I say as usual.

But Bella does not listen. "I like this card. I want it this way!" She is stubbornly pushing the card trying to lock it in place. The card resists, and she forces it sideway scratching the edges of both cards.

"See, what you have done! You hurt the poor little cards. And look at the trees! Do you want them to grow upside down?"

"Y-a-a-a," Bella says cunningly and goes on pushing another card. This one is engaged, but very loosely. "See, it fits!" The pumpkin looks at me triumphantly.

"No, it does not. And look, the river is flowing up the hills now. Try another card, please."

"But I like it this way! This way is better!" Bella insists.

She knows that trees in her yard do not grow topsy-turvy, and a waterfall in a local park does not run uphill. But she thinks that her way to play this game is better than that we taught her; that by changing the rules she makes the game more exciting and more fun for both of us.

"Fine, go on. Let's see what a picture you will get at the end."

It does not take long before Bella realizes that her way of playing this game is not better. A grotesque picture appearing on the cards is not as beautiful as what she sees around her in the yard, in the park and the books every day. She realizes that she made the castle levitate; forced the river to flow back; flattened the hills; and made the sun shine upside down. It is not fun after all. She grabs the cards, mixes them up and starts playing the game again—the right way this time, as it was intended by the game creator.

"Bella, it is lunch time!" My wife appears in the doorway. But Bella does not want to quit the game. She does not want to go downstairs and eat either. After some persuasion, Bella reluctantly stops playing, and they both walk downstairs together dancing and singing "Twinkle, twinkle little star."

Is this Just a Game?

I am lying on my back on the floor among a bunch of Bella's games and toys. I am thinking about my long and eventful life and a new tiny leaflet mysteriously growing right in front of my eyes. A perfect creation of Nature, a human life, is like a piece of chain—Nature holds one end; you grab another end at birth. Every link of that chain is an event in your life, and you are climbing up one link at a time until you reach the Nature's end.

There are so many events in our lives. Some of them are big and affect you directly and profoundly, while most of them are seemingly unrelated and unremarkable. They come and go unnoticed. You do not have time and desire to think about them, anyway. If you do, you do not take them seriously.

Like the cards Bella just assembled or like Bella's behavior during the puzzle-game. Why does a small child believe that her way of playing this game is better than that intended by the game creator? Why did Bella revolt against the rules of the game she played many times before and knew so well? Did the ugly picture she got make her come to her senses eventually? And will she repeat her mistake again?

I have this feeling that this is more than just a game I am thinking about. I am thinking about Life and Nature. Strange as it may seem, but Bella's behavior in playing this puzzle-game resembles the difficult relationship between Man and Nature.

Really, Nature gave Man a deck of cards to play a puzzle-game called Life and taught Man to follow the rules. And Man has been playing this game with Nature by the rules ever since. Man cheers along with Nature when the right card is locked in place and enjoys benefits of the right decisions as a reward.

Then, Man learned the game so well that he became arrogant and conceited. And here come socialists. They feel that they are wiser than Nature; that they are capable of improving the game; and they expect that the picture at the end will be more beautiful than reality. They rebel against Nature and change the rules of the game. While pushing the cards one into another, even if they do not fit, they are scratching and destroying the cards of Life in the process.

But what a disappointment! The picture expected at the end is a gross perversion of reality. Man finally abandons this socialist game at the end of the 20th century and returns to a free-market capitalist game playing by the rules created by Nature.

But will Man remember the lessons taught by Nature and for how long? Can Man learn his lessons at all? And here, the allegory Nature vs. Man is all about...

Incredible arrogance! Man has nerves to play against Nature that created the puzzle-game called Life challenging her eternal rules. In comparison with Nature, Man is not a mature adult; Man is not even an adolescent. If life on Earth since the emergence of multicellular life (1 billion years ago) had been compressed into one year, then Man as we know it today (since Neanderthals died out 25,000 years ago) would have been around for only...13 minutes! How can a newborn understand Nature's intentions? How can an infant play a game against an old grand master Nature?

In fact, this is not just a game; this is a war-game Man has been waging against Nature for several centuries since the Enlightenment era. The event used to justify the war (casus belli) has been the rapid advances in science, technology and medicine. The result is a powerful and euphoric feeling that Man is superior to Nature; Man is above Nature; Man is not part of Nature any more.

But is that so? Is the wisdom of Man superior to the wisdom of Nature?

Interview with Nature

Oh, I am fantasizing again! It is quiet and nap-provoking in Bella's bedroom. I stretch out on the floor and close my eyes. Bella will be away for at least an hour, so I can relax and keep on fantasizing. Is the wisdom of Man truly superior to the wisdom of Nature? If it is, then the products of a human mind have to be superior to those created by Nature.

Personally, I believe in limitless power of a human mind; its insatiable curiosity and unstoppable perseverance. As a scientist, I have enormous admiration for Man's tremendous achievements. Man is learning the laws of Nature and daring to venture way beyond the Nature's limits on land, in the water and air. Just look around—here are the products of human minds—cars, submarines, airplanes, spacecrafts, robots, computers, to name a few. Are these achievements superior to those of Nature? Most of us would agree that they are.

But what would Nature say if I ask her this question? There is only one way to find out: I have to interview Nature face to face. Well, Nature has always been generous to Man answering countless questions asked by curious human minds.

And here, I am standing in the office of the Almighty Nature, the Creator of every living creature, including Man. To my astonishment, the office is small and modest; a frugal, business surrounding; no fancy furniture; no secretary and no lawyer present.

"We have no budget for luxury, Man," says Nature intercepting my wide-eyed glance. "So, you think that Man is superior to Nature," Nature looks at me curiously and smiles.

"Sort of," I reply nervously looking in my handy notes for the first question.

"Do you agree that Man is the fastest creatures on land?" I begin my interview. "Nature gave Man legs to run, but Man

invented a wheel and runs faster than any land creature created by Nature now."

"So, you think that cars will win a race against land animals. Do you realize that Nature made animals run on off-road terrain, while cars need roads? Anyway, what are the fastest cars built by Man?"

"The fastest on-road car Ferrari[1] runs at *298 km/hr,* and the fastest all-terrain vehicle Platune-Sand-X[2] runs at *186 km/hr,*" I say with confidence and self-esteem.

"Is that all?" Nature says skeptically. "Even a cat runs faster. Cheetah[3] runs at *112 km/hr* (70 mph)."

"...But the cat runs slower than..." I am slightly confused.

"It does appear that way, absolutely," Nature says. "But relatively to its size, it does not. To compare apple to apple, we have to look at a speed-to-size ratio. In a second, a 4.5-m long Ferrari running at 83 m/sec covers the distance of *18* its body lengths, while a 1.24-m long cat running at 31 m/sec covers *25* its body lengths. So, relative to its size, the cat runs almost 40% faster on uneven ground than Ferrari does on a paved road!

To reach Cheetah's speed-to-size ratio, Ferrari has to run at...*413 km/hr* (258 mph) off-road! Comparison of the fastest ATV with the cat is also pathetic. Man has to learn a lesson or two from Nature before entering such race," Nature says with a good-natured smile.

"That was a neat trick," slightly embarrassed, I try to find the next question on my list.

"Do you agree that Man is the fastest swimmer under water?" I asked with less enthusiasm than before. "Man invented submarines to swim under water with tremendous speeds. One of them swims at 83 km/hr[4]—much faster than any marine creature created by Nature."

"This is not accurate, my friend. The Soviet nuclear submarine you have in mind was unique and scrapped long ago. Anyway, fish can swim faster. An ordinary Sailfish[5] swims at 112 km/hr, almost 30% faster. But look at its speed-to-size ratio: in one second, the submarine covers the distance of about *1/5th of* its body length, while the fish covers more than *10* its body lengths.

So, relatively to its size, the fish is about 47 times faster. To achieve the speed-to-size efficiency of the fish, a nuclear submarine should swim at...3,835 km/hr (2,397 mph)! I doubt Man will ever win this underwater race even if Man takes lessons from Nature. Next question!

"Do you think Man is the fastest flier?" I start feeling doubts about progress of mankind. "Being a crawling creature in the past, Man invented airplanes and space crafts, the marvels of a human mind. Now, Man flies much faster than any flying creature created by Nature. Just look at the space shuttle[6] that flies at a mind-boggling speed of 28,000 km/hr."

"The shuttle is unique; only three aging ones are in existence. And the speed of this marvel can be viewed as mind-boggling only by a tiny human mind," Nature replies sarcastically. "A bird flies faster. A White-Throated Needletail[7] flies routinely at 168 km/hr (105 mph), and it is not unique – thousands and thousands of them are born every year. Just compare speed-to-size ratios of the Needletail (*224* body length/sec) and the shuttle (only *138* body length/sec).

"But the shuttle flies at a supersonic speed—the speed that will never be achieved by any bird," I say in desperation.

"This is true. But contrary to Man, Nature creates everything out of necessity, not curiosity or vanity. Even ancient people like Aristotle noticed that "Nature does nothing uselessly." What frugal Nature cannot afford is to be wasteful as

Man is—there are too many mouths to feed on the planet Earth. It would be extremely inefficient and outright wasteful for a living creature to move with a speed of sound. Bird's speed is just sufficient to secure their survival. Peregrine Falcon has a diving speed of 320 km/hr (200 mph), just enough to catch its prey. Otherwise, Nature would have created a supersonic Peregrine Falcon."

"This interview is becoming quite embarrassing," I am saying to myself having little confidence and self-esteem left by this time.

"Would you at least recognize that Man is the most extreme traveler?" I hope that this topic may tip the debate in Man's favor. Well, if there is a symbol of Man's emancipation from Nature, it must be fantastic voyages by airplanes and spacecrafts.

"Experimental airplane Voyager[8] flew 41,000 km without stopping!" I say triumphantly. "What flying creature can come even close to that record?"

"Again, Voyager was a unique airplane created out of Man's vanity," Nature remarks. "Only one airplane was built and placed in a museum after a single flight. Weighing 4,400 kg (most of it was fuel), Voyager had a pathetic distance-to-weight efficiency of only *9.45* km/kg.

Sorry, but a bird can fly further. Arctic Terns[9], modest migratory birds that replicate themselves by thousands every year, fly routinely from their breeding grounds almost half around the Earth. It covers a distance of 22,000 km, while weighing only 106 gram. Where is my calculator? Oh, here it is. If the Arctic Tern flies non-stop at least 10 hours a day at 100 km/hr, it will cover 1,000 km at an astonishing distance-to-weight efficiency of about 10,000 km/kg!

At Voyager's distance-to-weight efficiency (*9.45* km/kg), the bird has to fly less than…1 km to break the airplane record. On the other hand, can you imagine how far the Voyager could have traveled at the bird's efficiency? A whooping *44 million* km (27.5 million miles), almost 1/3 of a trip to the Sun! I would display the bird in a museum instead of the Voyager!

"But Man flew…" I mumble diffidently and stop realizing that this argument will not fly further than the others.

"Did you want to say that Man traveled to the Moon, which is much further than 41,000 km?" Nature has caught my aborted thought. "Let's see, the distance to the Moon is 384,000 km and the round trip is 768,000 km. Oh, this is even more pitiful comparison and pretty insulting one to the bird. Man had to build the Apollo-Saturn V^{10} space vehicle to cover such distance. Weighing 3 million kg, Apollo had an appalling distance-to-weight efficiency of about *0.26* km/kg. At the efficiency of the Arctic Tern (10,000 km/kg), Apollo could've flown as far as *30 billion km* (*19 billion* miles) to the stars!"…stars…stars…

"Twinkle, twinkle, little Star," a familiar song interrupts the interview sparing me from further embarrassment and humiliation. Bella is marching back from lunch. It is time for my wife to take her to bed for a nap. I apologize and thank Nature for the interview.

"Children, you know," I shrug my shoulders.

"I know, you are all my children," Nature drives the last nail into the coffin where all my arguments are resting dead.

Are Wheels Really Superior to Legs?

Now, I need to leave Bella's bedroom promptly before she catches me up there. Otherwise, she will ask me to play games again instead of going to bed. I sneak downstairs to the kitchen and sit on the sofa next to Smokey, the cat, while Max, a 110-lb

German shepherd, coils up next to me on the floor. What an ideal atmosphere for thinking and fantasizing about Nature!

I am still digesting my imaginable, but sobering "interview" with Nature that has seriously shaken my confidence in Man's unlimited abilities and the progress achieved. The wisdom of Nature defied human comprehension and dwarfed Man's accomplishments. The miracles of Life created by Nature were evident in every animal, fish or bird.

In fact, Charles A. Lindbergh was the first man who flew like a migratory bird and probably felt like one when he was crossing the Atlantics. He had a lot of reasons to say: "In wilderness, I sense the miracle of life, and behind it our scientific accomplishments fade to trivia."

In fact, Man is bragging about many wonders of science and technology, but many of them are based on the principles invented by Nature millions of years before Man. Rockets are built on the principles that propel an octopus, while helicopters are a pitiful copy of a dragon fly. Agriculture was invented by ants growing fungus underground on decaying tree leaves, while spiders build a net from materials stronger than steel. Submarines use a primitive version of dolphin's sonar; the shape of aircraft wings was clumsily copied from those of birds; antibiotics are a gracious gift to Man from fungus; and so on.

Motion on wheels, the myth heralded as the greatest Man's invention of all times, appears to be the most primitive and the least economical way of motion. Sorry, but this is the only solution available to a limited human mind. Man has to build vehicles and infrastructure (roads, bridges, garages, oil rigs, gas stations, parking lots, etc.) to utilize wheels. Even with the aid of modern computers, artificial intelligence and advanced materials, Man is not capable of reaching the level of complexity and efficiency of...legs. Legs are an unimaginable, universal motion mechanism created by Nature for land animals to allow them to run fast on any terrain; to climb trees, steep rocks and cliffs. Nature did not even consider wheels to be a viable alternative to legs, I guess.

Another myth is a fixed-wing concept of flying, which is also considered as one of the most genius recent inventions of Man. It also appears to be the most primitive and the least economical way of flying. Sorry, but this is the only way of flying available to a limited human mind! Airplane created by Man cannot come even close to reaching the level of complexity and efficiency of flapping-wing birds and insects created by Nature. Just look at a cumbersome, metal-heavy, hollow wing of an airplane with an elegant, feathery-light wing of a dragon fly that consists of millions of extremely strong microscopic chambers filled with air.

And here is the super myth about Man's superiority over Nature—computers. The computing power (instructions per second) of modern computers doubles every couple of years (Time, Feb 21, 2011). The proponents of "Singularity" (the advent of superhuman intelligence) claim that computer may reach brain power of a mouse in 2015 and that of a human in 2023. They believe that a computer with artificial intelligence superior to the human brain is imminent. But there is more than just computing power needed. Nature created a human brain of incredible complexity, flexibility and efficiency; Nature-Creator allows Man to have consciousness and think in abstract categories. Man will be able t*o duplicate all that in a computer only if he becomes Creator!*

What in the world are you thinking about, Man? Nature gave you intelligence just to play Nature, not to become one! Nature has a safety valve to make sure it will never happen— Man's self destruction. "Man is the only living species that have the power to act as his own destroyer," Ayn Rand[11] said once.

True! Nature gave boundless curiosity to Man to discover fire, but cautioned Man to use it wisely.

"Hey, Man! Before trying to duplicate the entire Man's brain, try to reproduce much simpler things first, like...*a cell*, one of those 100 trillion residing in your body."

The Cell Tells it All

The cell is the unit of Life, the fundamental block of every living thing created by Nature on Earth. For Man peering through a primitive optical microscope less than two centuries ago, cell seemed to be very simple for understanding—it looked as a tiny lump of gelatin with a dark nucleus inside. But the more the cell was studied, the more complex and less understandable this microscopic living organism became.

Now, when we can see on almost molecular level, the cell exploded into Man's face as an enormously complicated, interlocking biological system that defies comprehension—a microscopic Universe created by Nature. And this is only the beginning of the endless road in understanding the structures and functions of a cell.

When you learn what is currently known about cell, nothing prepares you for the complexity of a giant (on a microscopic scale) self-contained factory called Cell. As a real factory run by Man, each cell consists of numerous specialized compartments ("shops")—shops storing and supplying genetic information (a complete set of body blueprints); shops generating energy; shops filled with biological machines producing, storing and transporting proteins; shops recycling and disposing waste and more.

The cell-factory is filled with thousands of assembly lines equipped with thousands of molecular protein-producing machines. A cell produces...millions of different proteins on a fantastic organizational level, which will never be achieved by Man!

But the most incredible thing is that cells can...replicate themselves! A cell is a factory that produces factories on a mass scale! Good Lord, how many years are needed to build an automobile assembly plant? But Nature cannot wait for so long—a cell replicates itself in minutes! Surprisingly, but Man has just vague ideas how this plant, shops and machines operate and interact; how they are controlled and organized.

As everything in a cell, some of these biological machines defy human imagination—like the flagellum, a rotary biological motor, which is attached to some cells to move them around. *A human sperm cell* is one of those cells.

A flagellum looks similar to a motor built by Man; it has a rotary engine; a tail that produces a propeller-like motion; a drive shaft; bushings, etc. Only it is made of various proteins. The flagellum is the smallest motor in existence (several microns in size). Its rotor spins at up to...17,000 rotations per minute (rpm) and, nevertheless, it can reach the maximum speed; reverse; or stop almost instantaneously (within one revolution). Man cannot even dream of that.

But this is not all! The motor propels some cells with the speed of...60 cell lengths per second!!! Man will never achieve such unthinkable efficiency and speed. Compare this speed with that of Cheetah, the world's fastest runner (25 body length/sec).

Even a 0.005-mm long human sperm cell swims at maximum speed of 0.050 mm/sec (Wikipedia, Sperm Cell) that is about 10 body length/sec. Unbelievable, but this tiny organism swims through thick mucus as fast as the world's fastest swimmer the Sailfish swims through water—at 112 km/hr (70 mph).

In other words, the inferiority of Man had never been as evident as when Man discovered and became familiar with the microscopic biological Universe called Cell. Man can only guess how it is designed; how it is organized; and what is the exact function of its numerous molecular machines and their products—proteins.

WHY DID MAN CHANGE THE RULES OF THE GAME?

So, is Man Superior to Nature?

Our ancestors kneeled before Nature in awe and bewilderment because they lived in the dark and knew too little. But not long ago, Man discovered magnetism, electricity, radioactivity, atomic structure, relativity of time and space. Man invented cars and spacecrafts; built huge skyscrapers and cities; factories and complex machines; even decoded the human genome trying to read the messages sent to Man from Nature.

But the more Man reads messages from Nature, the more he realizes how primitive his knowledge and achievements are in comparison with those of Nature; how limited are his abilities to comprehend what Nature has ingeniously created. If Man creates something that Nature does not, it means that Man does not know about it yet or Nature does not need it.

"If one way be better than another, that you may be sure is nature's way," the great Greek philosopher Aristotle said more than two millenniums ago. It is true today, and it will be true tomorrow.

In fact, the marvels of science and technology have always been achieved by studying laws of Nature and trying to utilize the acquired knowledge for their developments. Despite enormous vanity, Man is still in his infancy. Man just scratches the surface of the world created by Nature. Man looks at it, but cannot see it; trying to explain it, but cannot comprehend it.

Now, modern Man has returned to square one. Again, Man kneels before Nature in awe and astonishment. In a paradoxical way, Man is still living in the dark and still knows little. Like a diligent student, Man is trying to study the most spectacular inventions of Nature implemented in land and marine animals, fish, birds and insects; trying to learn from Nature and duplicate those inventions (on a very primitive level, of course, and not always successfully).

Scientists are studying an amazing structure of dolphin's skin to make submersibles swim faster and more efficiently; a human brain to develop artificial intelligence; animal's muscular-skeleton system to make robots walk. They try to learn how Nature made animals see, hear and smell so unbelievably good; birds and insects fly, maneuver in the air and navigate during migration so amazingly; dolphins locate objects under water with such precision using their superb sonar; and so on.

In other words, Man has conceded to Nature. Man is trying diligently and enthusiastically to comprehend the fundamental rules of the puzzle-game called Life.

Rules of Life? What are You Talking About?

If Life is governed by some fundamental rules created by Nature, those are probably the rules that allowed Life to exist and flourish on Earth for millions of years.

Living creatures need energy. They obtain it from vital resources (food, water, oxygen). The cells convert the resources into energy and building materials, which allow the living creatures to grow and develop; to respond to their environment and evolve (slowly change) in response to any changes in the environment.

No resources—cells die. That's too bad because cells reproduce only from other cells. No one knows where the first cell has come from, but everyone knows that, if the last cell dies, Life on Earth will never resume; it will end for ever. So, if you are a mother, what would you care about before anything else in the world? Your baby! So does Nature! As her first priority, Mother-Nature cares about her baby—LIFE! Nature PRESERVES LIFE at any cost!

But how did Nature manage to sustain life for so long? Well, Nature deliberately made all living creatures from mortal cells, but ingeniously armed them with a powerful tool of immortality—the ability to reproduce and pass their traits onto their offspring. So, paraphrasing Shakespeare, I would say: "Life is a stage, and the Sperm Cell is the major player." And what a player! What an Oscar-winning performance in the leading role category!

Why did Nature make a sperm cell one of the most fascinating, enduring, efficient and the fastest living thing in existence? It is because sperm cells ORIGINATE AND REPRODUCE LIFE!

In a way, sperm cell is Her Majesty Life Itself! If some fundamental rules of Life exist in Nature, a sperm cell will probably follow them in its behavior. If Nature wishes to convey a message to Man about the rules of Life, a sperm cell will probably be the Nature's Confidant and the most trusted Messenger. Let's watch sperm cells behavior and try to interpret those messages about the rules of Life.

Rule 1—No Free Ride. Nature did not make all sperm cells equal in strength, stamina or speed, but millions of participating cells are given an equal opportunity to get the egg. Figuratively speaking, all the cells start their runs from the same scratch line and at the same time—no favors and no free rides. And, boy, they are running! They put up everything they've got to the last breath, so to speak.

This run is an exhausting test—they are swimming through thick acidic mucus inside a woman's womb. How far? Let's figure it out. The length of a sperm cell body is about 0.005 mm. If the cell moves as far as the fallopian tubes (assume about 100 mm away), then the relative distance will be about 20,000 cell bodies. If an average woman's height is 1.6 m

(5'4"), then this run is a human equivalent of swimming as far as…32 km (about 20 miles) through…an oil spill…at 112 km/hr (70 mph)!

What a deadly marathon! Why is there no free ride for at least some "less fortunate" cells? Man does it all the time for certain groups of runners sparing them from severe scrutiny of Nature, but not for the Navy S.E.A.L.s! Like sperm cells, they are subjected to a merciless, excruciating and cruel training exercise—no favors and no free rides. Oh, come on! This is different—lives are at stake. See, even Man behaves as a sperm cell if it is a matter of life or death.

So does Nature. Nature would never give a lift to a free rider; it would be detrimental to the preservation of Life. A poorly qualified sperm-cell candidate does not create Life; it ruins it.

When Man gives a free ride to some runners, it leaves the rest of the runners with little incentive to run hard. Opposite to Man, Nature has a drastically different attitude to incentives: it gives all sperm cells the highest incentive possible—Life!

If you can interpret such explicit behavior differently, good luck; but in my interpretation, the messages Nature sends to Man are

> *Life is about equal Opportunity—not Equality.*
> *Free rides ruin Life—they contradict Nature.*
> *Incentives are the driving force of Life.*

Rule 2—No Free Lunch. Hordes of sperm cells rush in search of just one egg trying to reach the egg first. Millions of swimmers are racing at the maximum speed to the finish line to win the ultimate price—Life.

Imagine agonizing 32-km swim at 112 km/hr! This cruel competition with a staggering number of participants is an incredible test of vitality, vigor and stamina of each sperm cell. Why does Nature force the sperm cells to work so hard? It is because the winner inherits and continues Life! So, here are clear messages to Man:

Competition is the way of Life;
Every living creature must work hard to earn its keep.

Rule 3—No Altruism. When the winner sperm cell reaches and penetrates the egg, it starts shouting loudly: "This egg is mine! I earned this egg! I will not share it with anyone! I will defend it at any cost!" This is not a bluff or an empty threat. The winner triggers a mechanism that erects an impenetrable wall around the egg instantaneously to keep off other cells.

Think about the logic of Nature. Why is a sperm cell, the embodiment of Life, so egoistic? Why does it hold its self-interest above the interests of others? Why it does not share the egg with other sperm cells altruistically? Man does it all the time, even at risk of ruining Life. But Nature does not allow another sperm cell into the egg because it means the end of Life. Nature is against altruism. So, the messages to Man are

Living creature must own, keep and protect what they earn;
Self-interest is the way of Life;
Altruism contradicts Nature.

These are the messages Nature sends to Man "from a sperm cell's mouth"—the messages about the fundamental rules of Life. I would have dismissed these messages as my fantasy, but I cannot find other explanations. Honestly, I would, but such behavior is observed not only in sperm cells. All living things in Nature live by the same eternal rules also. Otherwise, Life would have ceased to exist long ago. Those defying these rules are doomed to disappear sooner or later. Those obeying these rules are destined to live and propagate—they are insured by Nature.

Then, why in the world, Man wants to get rid of these rules of Nature? There is the only one plausible, but frightening explanation: MAN DOES NOT CARE ABOUT PRESERVATION OF LIFE AS NATURE DOES!

The Turkey Rule

"Woo-f...Woo-f...Woo-o-f!" Loud and powerful barking suddenly wakes me up. God damn it, Max—it is 5:30 in the morning! I come downstairs. The dog is peering through the window into the woody yard in the rear of the house. His ears bigger then my palm are sticking up as well as his hair.

"Max! No barking!" I come to the window to investigate; I know Max never barks at nothing.

Oh, my God! Wild turkeys are roaming over there between the trees. One, two, three...four of them! I have never seen a turkey in the wild, only on TV. Look at their posture! Look at how dignified, magnificent and free these birds are! What a contrast to their domesticated, fat, locked up relatives—a symbol of laziness and stupidity!

"How did you, guys, get here? For God's sake, you are 17 miles from New York!"

"We came here from far away—there is no *free ride* for us in the wild. Free ride is only for the domesticated, lazy relatives of ours that travel in comfortable trailers...to a meat factory!"

"What are you doing here that early in the morning in the yard owned by a 110-lb German shepherd?"

"We have to come early ahead of *competition* and *work hard* all day long *taking risk*. Food is hard to come by and there is no *free lunch* for us in the wild. Free lunch and no competition are only for the fatty relatives of ours that have to gain a lot of weight in crowded, stuffy chicken coops rapidly ...before Thanksgiving!"

"Have you heard, Max? Although you are a domesticated beast, you should still remember the rules of Life!"

And Max does remember. He is furious: the turkeys have invaded the territory the dog *owns and protects*. But, the birds, which are extremely cautious in the wild, do not fly away and seemingly don't give a damn about the angry beast. They keep on foraging tirelessly for food in the ground.

"Get off my private property, dumb turkeys!" Max is roaring. But the wild turkeys are not dumb: obviously, they know that this is an empty threat—the dog is locked up. They snub the dog: "This is the wild turkey rule, stupid: *If you cannot defend your property, it is not yours!*"

H-mm...I never thought about this rule. I sit on the sofa. Max comes and puts his head on my laps. He stops barking; he understands the turkey rule. I see it in his intelligent amber eyes questioning me and in his pricked ears expecting me to say that I understand it too.

"I understand, Max. This is a rule of Life, the law of Nature, which is applicable equally to both dogs and Man. I was not aware of this rule when I lived in the former USSR; I was locked up and there were no private property rights there. In the US where I live now, I just take it for granted—my property rights are protected by laws and defended by others. And it will always stay this way."

Max looks at me and pricks his ears again.

"What, Max? You don't believe that it will always stay this way...Maybe you are right, Max. If we do not defend our property every single day; if we become too ignorant, lazy and fat; then one day, the Turkey rule will kick in, and our property will be taken away. I know what it means to be a domesticated turkey locked up in a small, stuffy chicken coop.

Thanks you so much, dear wild turkey, for giving me and Max such an educational lesson on obeying the rules of Life. What a pity that Man does not understand what even a turkey does. What a pity that a turkey cannot give a lecture or two at an Ivy League university about the rules of Life! "

Rules of Life: Chaos or Order?

Living in the USSR, I got used to a tight supervision and a rigid society structure; to a strict order and meticulous planning. In this respect, life of living things in Nature looked like real anarchy, disarray and disorder. My head was spinning from questions.

How do myriads of living things, big and small, find a place to live; food to eat; water to drink; opposite sex to mate? Why does not Nature provide any apparent guidance or help? Why do all creatures work so hard all day long when there is no apparent coercion from Nature? Why are fierce competition and rivalry between them encouraged by Nature when all this can be avoided through rationing and distribution? Why does Nature allow all living things to roam free anywhere and live wherever they want without any permission and supervision? And why, in the world, they are allowed to claim anything they find as their own without any approval?

Is Nature smart enough? It looks like an incredible blunder to allow all living things to do whatever they want. Eventually, such mayhem had to make life impossible on Earth: grazing animals had to graze off all the grass by now; the predators had to wipe out the entire population of grazers; stinky litter, waste and decay had to suffocate the planet. Is this bad management on the part of Nature? Where is the planning and regulations in replenishment of vital resources; in controlling the population growth; in keeping Earth in decent, sanitary conditions? There are no planning, no regulations whatsoever in these jungles on the planet Earth! Just chaos!

Yet, there has been no chaos in Nature! On the contrary, a miracle has happened: out of this chaos, *a perfect order emerged called Life.* Myriads of living creatures, from huge mammals to bacteria, are interconnected and dependent on each other. They managed to live in perfect harmony with their natural environment; to regulate, sustain, reproduce and recycle themselves for millions of years without the apparent interference from Nature. If there is an abundance of food, population grows; if food is in short supply, population declines. Rivals know when and where to compete for territory, resources and mates. Animals, insects and bacteria themselves carry out waste management. In the summer time, a bear is active and gorges itself to gather extra fat, while, during winter, it is dormant and lives off its fat to wait out. Every living creature knows its niche, its place, its role and what it has to do.

It is like an invisible baton without a conductor conducts a world-class symphony orchestra; the world-class professional musicians are playing masterpieces of classical music; they play by heart in absolute harmony and with consummate mastery.

When I came to the US from the USSR, my head was spinning from questions too. No matter how often I talked to my neighbor, a small business owner, I could not grasp how this strange free-market system could practically work.

What do you mean you have to fend for yourself? Doesn't the Government provide any help or at least guidance? No?

Then, who told you to open a grocery store? No one? No wonder you have to work 12 hours a day! Oh, everyone is working that hard if he wants to succeed in life!

What do you mean you want to open another grocery store? Why do you have to take such risk—there is another grocery nearby, your competitor?

Oh, if you don't do it, your competitor will do it, anyway!

But how can you be sure that you will have enough customers and supplies? You are not sure, are you?

Then, what if you are low or high on supplies? Oh, you will expand or shrink right away, and your suppliers will do the same!

What do you mean you have to drive your competitor out of business before he does? Oh, you will give his customers much better deal!

What are you going to do if he drives you out of business? Oh, you will be fine working for somebody else. Oh, every one does it if he is unable to run a business himself.

Why, in the world, are you allowed to own two stores, anyway? What do you mean anyone can open and own any number of stores anywhere he wants and can sell anything he wants? Absolute madness and chaos!

So, who is planning how many customers are out there; how many stores and supplies are needed? How much does everyone need? No one at all?

...Oh, my God, there is a jungle out there! Millions of various businesses are popping up everywhere like gas bubbles in the boiling water. They are buying and selling blindly and uncontrollably whatever they want. The majority of them are struggling to survive, and only few survive and prosper (as in Nature). Competing vigorously, they are driving each other out of business (like rivals do in Nature). Where are those people who care, who try to regulate or stop this mess? Nobody gives a damn (like in Nature). In other words, people are allowed to run aimlessly in every direction without supervision and do whatever they want without permission. Such a waste of human and material resources is not supposed to lead to prosperity.

But here is a miracle: instead and out of this anarchy, *not really perfect, but a decent order emerges.* This order allows this chaotic free-market system to provide an abundance of everything; to produce what people need and can afford! Without interference from the Government, people are able to produce and sell; regulate and sustain themselves as all living things in Nature. The only "worry"—such system may produce too much. But if it does, it slows down and lives off its abundance like a bear lives off its fat in the winter time in Nature. Although this order is not as perfect as that in Nature, most of the niches are filled, and the vast majority of people find their place, their role and what they have to do. They do it themselves without guidance and supervision; without permission and approval; without rationing and distribution as it is done in Nature.

It is like an invisible baton without a conductor conducts a modest local community band (rather than a world-class symphony orchestra). Here, amateur musicians (rather than world-class professionals) are playing simple pop songs (rather than masterpieces of classical music). They play from music sheets (not by heart)...well, in some dissonance, but fairly well—much better than any local band in the human history.

In other words, *this chaotic capitalist, free-market system borrows its ideas from Nature; it imitates Nature and the rules of Life as close as a limited human mind is capable of doing!*

What a striking difference with the planned, socialist system in the USSR where I grew up. Every aspect of life was planned by others there. A seemingly perfect order was achieved through guidance and supervision; permission and approval; rationing and distribution. People were told where to live; what and how much to eat, drink and dress; what and how many things to produce; and many other things like that. No one owned anything; and no competition was necessary. Instead of running aimlessly all over the place, everyone was marching in one direction—no apparent waste. Isn't this the way to prosperity? Perfect order and no chaos!

Then, why in the world, was such an orderly system not able to provide enough food and necessities people need and can afford? Why there was so little progress in science, technology and industry in comparison with chaotic capitalist free-market world?

It is like an amateur conductor (who is not even a musician) conducts a high school band where students (who could hardly play their instruments) are not provided with music sheets and do not know the music by heart. The result is not music, but cacophony.

Now, I understand—*this "orderly" socialist system is artificial and unnatural; it is misguided and disorganized; it contradicts Nature and ignores the rules of Life!*

In other words, humanity is gradually descending moving away from the legacy of Nature from slavery, feudalism and to free-market capitalism. While the free-market system still lives by the rules slightly resembling those of Nature and enjoys the benefits, the socialist system is a quantum leap...down the precipice where Nature's eternal laws and rules of Life are flatly rejected—they are replaced with the Man-made artificial laws and rules that do not exist in Nature.

Does Man Obey the Rules of Life?

For millenniums, Man followed the rules of Life by working hard; by competing for resources; by keeping and protecting what Man earned as private property.

But not long ago, Man decided to revolt against and defy Nature. Man decided that he learned how to organize the structure of a human society better than Nature does. And Man changed the rules of Life. In a short blip of human history, by breaking the laws of Nature, Man tried to make "the world a better place to live" without hardship, competition and private property. That is exactly what happened in the 19th and 20th centuries, the era of socialist ideals and practice.

Although the ideals of socialism were disseminated by ancient philosophers like Plato who believed in a society where "the private and individual will be altogether banished from life," the seeds of socialism were planted in the 19th century by Karl Marx, while Vladimir Lenin and his followers grew these seeds into poisonous plants that spread around the world in the 20th century. Karl Marx and Lenin believed that humanity is ascending from slave-owning system, feudalism and capitalism; eventually, it reaches the summit-socialism, which is the final, the most advanced and desired stage of the human societal evolution.

The ideals of socialism were presented and viewed as *Promised Land*, which Nature has never seen before; as an advanced and progressive society. These ideals were bold, appealing and promising. At least, I was taught this way in the former USSR where I have spent half of my life.

These ideals promised to create a society based on economic EQUALITY, which brings abundance and prosperity achieved through elimination of competition; through the abolition and expropriation of private property.

They promised to create a society based on ALTRUISM; a society, in which everyone is purged of natural acquisitiveness; in which everyone lives for others sacrificing one's own well being—a society of genuine freedom.

They promised to change HUMAN NATURE for the better by eradicating Man's inborn, primordial vices and by creating a superior Man through education. What can I say?

MAN, I LIVED IN THE PROMISED LAND!
THE PROMISED LAND WAS THE HOME OF MINE!
SOCIALISM IS NOT THE PROMISED LAND!

The ideals of socialism were first implemented in the USSR; the country which was euphorically portrayed as the Promised Land. But in practice, it was a perverted and horrific picture similar to that my 4-year old grand-daughter Bella obtained playing the puzzle-game.

In practice, socialism did not bring equality—everyone lived equally in poverty, except privileged few. In fact, socialism was an antipode of abundance and prosperity.

In practice, instead of altruistic and free society, socialism created a society of hungry and egoistic slaves secretly longing for freedom and material things due to lack of both.

In practice, instead of improving human nature, socialism corrupted, abused and raped human nature on an unthinkable scale. Socialists found a simple and efficient way to eradicate inborn human vices—they eradicated millions of people together with their vices in killing fields and hard-labor camps.

In other words, socialism created an artificial world where everything was upside down; where everything contradicted and insulted Nature and its creation—human nature. In a way, socialism was trying to build a new world, in which everything levitates defying the Nature's law of gravity.

So, there is an obvious contradiction in Man' attitude to Nature. On one hand, Man eventually realized the greatness of Nature; that Nature gives Man great inspiration and hope; that inventions of Nature should be studied, learned and duplicated to the best of Man's limited abilities for enormous benefits of Man. Now, Man kneels before Nature in awe and astonishment again as our ancient ancestors did.

On the other hand, Man arrogantly believes that he is superior to and above Nature; that the rules of Nature are too primitive, worthless, unsuitable and useless for Man to learn and follow; that the premises of these rules are wrong and unfair. Therefore, the unfair rules created by Nature must be replaced by new, fair rules created by a human mind in order to build a new, unprecedented social structure of a human society based on ECONOMIC EQUALITY, ALTRUISM; AND REJUVINATED HUMAN NATURE.

Wait a minute! This contradiction has already been resolved after the communist and socialist doctrines have catastrophically failed around the world. The ideals of socialism defied Nature and Nature did not allow these ideals to levitate; these ideals were doomed to disappear and they did disappear.

Now, the ideals of free-market capitalism have prevailed; the ideals which are based on competition, private property rights, self-interest and freedom to do what you like at your own risk—the ideals created, endorsed and sponsored by Nature, not a human mind.

But did the ideals of discredited socialism really disappear? Are they dead after sacrificing millions of human lives? Not at all! They are still alive. Rising from their grave, they are walking into our life like the living dead every day. We just do not pay much attention and do not see them coming because they are hidden behind noble causes of helping the poor; camouflaged as altruistic actions; and masqueraded as genuine manifestation of the best in human nature.

Sorry, but Man does not learn lessons from Nature or history after all—a mysterious paradox of a human mind…

Hey, what is the matter with you, man? You started playing an innocent puzzle-game with your grand-daughter and ended up wandering in the jungle of philosophy of Life. Wake up, man! Bella probably is up already. It is time for you to run upstairs and start a new puzzle game. And no philosophy this time!

Chapter 2
NATURE VS. EQUALITY

EQUALITY AND THE RICH

Fur Hat and Equality

It happened in Chicago in 1981, about two years after I immigrated to the US from the USSR. One cold winter morning, I was riding home in a cab from O'Hare airport after a business trip. Suddenly, I noticed that the cab driver, a young American, was watching me in the mirror with interest. Then, he asked:

"Sir, are you from Russia?"

"Yes, I am. How did you find out, by my accent?"

"No, Sir, it's your fur hat. All Russians wear them. My college professor told us that the Russians were very wealthy. The Government gives everyone a big salary; a free house; free education in colleges; free health care; and other things. There are no millionaires; everyone is equal in the USSR. Is this true?

"Yes, this is true. Everyone is equal in the USSR, the socialist Land of Equality."

"Sir, tell me more, please!" The driver was so agitated that almost lost control of the car.

"Sure, let's start with "big" salaries. The Government is the only employer in the country. It decides whom to pay and how much. So, it pays about the same "big" salary to everyone, a cab-driver or a doctor. Fortunately or not, the Government does not tell you how much you actually earn and how much they keep without your consent either (90-95%, I guess). What you bring home is just enough for you to buy some food to prevent you from starving and some clothes. After that, there is little left for anything else from that "big" salary. You live from salary to salary feeling that they can pull a plug on your life any moment if they want to.

"Do you want to hear about free houses too? The Government is the only landlord in the country. Since they own all real estate, they have no choice, but to provide a shelter (not a house, of course) for you and your family. Otherwise, everyone would be homeless. Typically, for a small token fee, they allow you to rent a room in a communal (hotel-type) apartment where you share a kitchen and a toilet with 3-6 other families. But you have to stay on a waiting list for 5-10 years to get it. (Only in 1959, when Nikita Khrushchev has learned how ordinary Americans live during his visit to the US, he started housing development in the USSR after more than 40 years of neglecting people's needs).

About education? The Government owns all schools and colleges. Since you have no money to pay for education, the Government has to pay teachers—they need people who can read and write. They have to pay also college professors to educate you—they need teachers and engineers. But the Government decides whom to accept in colleges by quotas. Accepted are only those who believe in Marxism; 50% quota— for workers; 25 %—for peasants; 3%—for Jews, etc. Having good grades and talent are not enough. The Government (not you) decides where you should go to work after graduation too—typically, against your wishes.

About health care? The Government owns all hospitals and pharmacies, but you have no money to pay for your health care. So, they have to pay the doctors and nurses to keep you well and prevent you from getting sick and die. In fact, you may die before you get an operation waiting for many months for permission. You may get even sicker like my father after he got his ulcer removed. There were 30 patients in a recovery room and only one nurse on duty. You may get an infection from lack of care like my mother-in-law when she was recovering after a breast-cancer operation. If you need post-medical care after an operation, you'd better buy drugs on a black market; the hospitals do not have enough drugs for everyone. The Government also designates a doctor to treat you as long as you or your doctor lives.

Shall I tell you about other things? Fine! Did your college professor tell you that the Russians are equal in having no property rights? You were not supposed to have a car. If you do, you are a suspected thief and the Government will audit your finances. You cannot own anything: a house or apartment; a truck or a taxi cab; any tools to make any product for sale.

Did your professor tell you that the Russians are equal in having no elementary human rights? You cannot work for yourself; you cannot reside, work or travel where you want without Government's permission. You cannot criticize the Government; if you do, you will find yourself at a mental institution or a uranium mine (along with your lawyer if you find one)...Shall I tell you more about the land of social and economic Equality?"

"No, Sir, I've got the visuals. Thank you very much."

I was thinking about that conversation and my previous life in the USSR. From ancient time, many thinkers were trying to find the *Promised Land or Utopia* where people could achieve economic equality; get rid of egoism, greed, envy and other natural vices.

Plato outlined the ideals—the Promised Land should be the Land of Equality where people would "remove the fences that separate yours and mine." Carl Marx laid out these ideals on a map to show how to get there: by expropriating property of the rich. And Vladimir Lenin found the Land of Equality using this map and by putting Marx's ideas into practice in Russia.

Many thinkers were dreaming about economic equality over millenniums. But was this elusive goal was achieved in the Land of Equality? It is true that USSR was the only place on Earth where the rich were banned, at least legally. It is true that everyone had as much of material things as others did, almost as much. But no economic equality was achieved; the price paid was too high; and the brutal, deadly sacrifice was not worth it.

Why are the Rich Called Filthy?
Man is created equal before God, or before Law. Man has inalienable rights for Life, Liberty and the pursuit of Happiness. This is the foundation of social justice and social equality in the US. Then, why in their pursuit of happiness, people become unequal economically? Why are they separated by their weight in a huge centrifuge of Life?

Let me say this bluntly: people love to possess material things. No matter how much we donated this year, acquisitiveness inside us is an undisputable fact. Look at the people's faces distorted from avarice on Oprah's shows "My Favorite Things" where a give-away of free stuff is going on an obscene scale. Those are primordial faces of our ancestors.

Who wants to be a millionaire? Everyone! Well, except billionaires. Ask your family, friends and countrymen, anyone on this planet—nobody wants to be homeless. You have a dollar—you want two; you have two million—you want three. It is likely we are born this way—Nature sets the rules and makes people acquisitive.

Even in the former USSR! For 70 years, the Soviet people were forcibly instructed to defy Nature: to be selfless and to despise material things. Greed or envy was viewed as a shameful venereal disease. But even there, inequality in possession of material things was still openly evident breeding greed and envy.

The ruling class (communist party nomenclature) was supplied in secret distribution centers, in abundance, while the rest of the population stood in lines for hours to get every necessity. And the monthly salaries of the nomenclature were much higher than those of ordinary people. Such inequality was outrageous.

Do you call it outrageous? What a crock! When I came to the US and started watching the TV series "Lifestyles of Rich and Famous" narrated by Robin Leach (all those jaw-dropping mansions, eye-popping yachts, flashy jewelry), only then I realized how unjust I was to my old socialist country. Compared to the US, it was the shining monument of unmolested economic *Equality*. I also realized what capitalist economic *Inequality* really means. After watching that TV show, every decent heart was supposed to boil against the rich and inequality they create.

Filthy rich, how often we hear this cliché? Of course, most people have never been in a shower with a rich guy to verify this fact. We do not know how they became rich, and we don't care. What we feel that there is some kind of illegitimacy and filth associated with being rich. Thanks a lot to our progressive media for that. You also feel that you should have at least as much of material things as your neighbor has. As long as your neighbor has more, this is a very appealing, heart-warming and progressive feeling.

Whenever the word "rich" comes to mind, the adjective "filthy" sticks to it like a magnet as well as others like unequal, egoistic, greedy, unjust, unfair, selfish, illegitimate (our media is extremely resourceful). We have been bombarded with these stereotypes, not in the USSR, but here, in the US every day. And no wonder (why pretend), to bring one of the rich guy down or to justice is a very appealing, heart-warming and progressive thought.

But Equality is another story. The concept of Equality has always been revered as sacred and untouchable. Its facade is shiny, urging to follow, calling, inspiring, euphoric, intoxicated and most important...promising. It promises a new, better life; abundance instead of misery; spirituality instead of materialism; altruism instead of envy and greed; and freedom—real freedom.

Are these promises too good to be true? Do they sound like a dream or a fairytale? In fact, the most memorable fairytales are about the rich and the poor, the poor being always triumphant over the rich.

Fisherman and Golden Fish

This is the name of a famous fairytale written by Alexander Pushkin, the Great Russian poet of the 19th century. I used to read it to my daughter at bedtime when she was small. As many fairytales, this one was also emotionally and socially charged, and cries out against inequality. It goes like this.

Once upon a time, there lived an old, poor fisherman. He lived in a mud-hut with his old lady. She was a laundress washing filthy linen (for rich people, I guess). The only valuable possession they had was a cracked, wooden tub (case against inequality). One day, the old man caught a strange fish. Her scales were made of pure gold, and she could speak. "Let me go, the Golden Fish begged, and I will fulfill all your wishes." But the old man was not greedy (case against acquisitiveness) and let her go asking nothing for himself (altruism).

When he returned home and told this amazing story to his wife, she was furious. "Go back and ask the Golden Fish to replace my cracked tub." And the Golden Fish replaced the tub. But the tub was not enough for the old lady. She demanded more and more freebies from the Golden Fish—a house, a mansion and a prestigious title of nobility (greed). And the Golden Fish kept her word. Eventually, the old laundress was turned into a Queen living in a marble palace (vanity), while the old man had to stay in his mud-hut. (Now, you feel nothing, but revulsion toward the rich).

This shameless spectacle continued until … the new Queen wished the Golden Fish to become a servant of hers. But this time, the Golden Fish did not say a single word to the old man (I could think of two). She just swam away for good. The old man went back to his mud-hut. And look, who was there? His old lady was there washing linen in a cracked tub. (At this point, everyone is ready to drown the old bitch in her tub).

I was thinking about the sense of this fairytale often. I always interpreted it as a truly educational lesson in excessive greed and its consequences. Later, I realized that it had a hidden philosophical underlining that eluded me for so long. In fact, the tale describes allegorically the relationship between Man (the old laundress) and Nature (the Golden Fish).

Rich or poor, Man behaves the same way: Man wants more and more. This is a human nature. Nature has always been generous and patient as long as Man doesn't ask Nature to serve at the table. Then, all bets are off, and all Man's efforts go to waste. The conclusion: if Man does things that abuse or insult Nature, Man will end up having nothing, but a cracked tub.

Wait a minute! What does this conclusion have to do with economic Equality? Do you mean that when people try to achieve economic equality they are abusing Nature?

Yes, I do! Like a great sculptor, Nature worked to develop and shape a human nature/character for millions of years. A perfect product of Nature, it is wired to work hard for its survival in competition with all living creatures without exceptions. There is no "free lunch" in Nature and, thus the *concept of Equality contradicts and corrupts human nature*!

DOES EQUALITY REALLY EXIST?

Does Equality Exist in Natural World or in Living Nature?

In fact, the concept of Equality is foreign to the natural world. Can you find any piece of land or lake equal in size or shape? Can you find any mountain or cloud? Even each piece of snowflakes or sand is different. Every spot of land or ocean, every bush or tree, receives unequal amount of solar energy, rain or wind. Soil fertility, spread of vegetation, mineral deposits—anything that sustains life or human activities is unequal. Think about it. What would happen if mineral resources were distributed evenly around the planet crust? No deposits of iron, coal or oil would be found anywhere! The only equal things that can be found on Earth are the products of human activities.

This is a manifestation of inequality in Nature governed by the laws of Nature. Life can be sustained and flourish if there is a gradient, an upward or downward slope. Rivers are flowing from a higher place to a lower place. Hot air and hot water are rising, while cold air and cold water are sinking. A hurricane is an enormous concentration of hot air and vapor in one spot. We hate hurricanes; they kill people and destroy properties. But they rapidly transfer huge masses of fresh and warm air, oxygen and moisture to distant, chilly, stuffy and thirsty lands like gigantic fans.

Gradients support Life. This principle has never been evident to proponents of Equality. In fact, for progressives or socialists who worship Equality, a gradient is a gruesome symbol of inequality; it is a foreign, disgusting and outright criminal concept. It does not fit into their theory of socio-economic justice.

The main premise of this theory is to eliminate inequality among humans. Is it possible? It is like to view the existence of hills and planes on Earth as inequality and injustice. Allegorically speaking, there is no place for hills in this theory. And in practice, the hills must be removed to level the playing field for all and to make the world a better (flatter) place to live.

But this is an absurdity. The rivers running from the hills will stop running, and the "leveled playing field" will turn into a muddy swamp deprived of oxygen and nutrients. Will the world be a better place where there is an abundance of mud and lack of oxygen; where everyone is *equally* in mud up to their ears?

The socialist theory defies Nature. *Inequality of the natural world is what supports life on Earth*—a fundamental premise of Nature*!*

No equality exists in living Nature either. All individual living creatures are different in size and shape: big and small; strong and weak; fast and slow. Every tree, branch or leave is different. Not a single, living thing is alike and equal. And the distribution of vital living resources among living creatures is also not equal. Due to this inequality, every living creature competes and works hard for its share. Due to this inequality, innumerous living creatures are compelled to interact; to find its place and its niche. Due to this inequality, living creatures manage to survive and propagate. Inequality is a wise Nature's strategy that allows the limited resources to be utilized to the fullest extent—nothing goes to waste in Nature. Due to this inequality, the living Nature managed to sustain itself for millions and millions of years without depleting scarce resources of a relatively small planet like Earth. The socialist theory of Equality defies Nature. *Inequality is the way of life of all living creatures*—a fundamental premise of Nature*!*

No equality ever existed in a human society either. Although people are created equal before Law, they are not created equal before Nature. Nature made them tall and short;

strong and weak; healthy and sick; hardworking and lazy; venturous and irresolute; intelligent and mentally challenged (retarded, for God's sake). How can it be natural that everyone is entitled to share natural resources equally regardless of contribution; without competing and working hard for it? The simple truth is that to make everyone live equally is possible, but to make everyone live both equally and comfortably is not.

Inequality is the law of Nature for any living creature, including Man. Yes, Man has always been a part of Nature even if it does not fit socialist theory of economic justice. There are fundamental differences how Man and Nature view the equality and inequality, apart of semantics.

Equality is the way Man thinks; inequality is the way Nature lives.

Equality exists in a human mind as a practical concept for two hundred years; Nature has been practicing inequality for millions of years.

For Man, Equality is an enlightened, appealing and desirable way of life; in contrast, Nature views Equality as an arrogant and destructive product of a human mind.

For Man, inequality is a primitive, outdated and repugnant obstacle in the way of progress; but for Nature inequality is a driving force of life.

The purpose of equality is more appealing to Man than the hidden purpose of inequality; but when it comes to the consequences, it is quite the opposite.

As will be shown later, despite the uplifting façade, Equality drags people down; it discourages competition; it punishes excellence and achievement. It makes people destroy what other people have already built. Every one loses at the end.

Inequality drives people up. It creates a powerful driving force that makes them compete, excel and achieve. Notorious wealth concentration is similar to a hurricane. It rapidly transfers enormous resources to build not only palaces and monuments, but industries, commerce and technology. Everyone benefits at the end. And the rich plays a crucial, disproportional role in creating this prosperity.

The neon-bright and sparkling facade of equality hides its dark appeal to primordial corners of human nature: to take away from others. Redistribution of extra fat is the only way equality can be achieved.

Look how a parasitic wasp operates. It paralyzes its victim; lays and hatches its eggs in the victim's fat body using its extra fat to feed wasp's larva. This cannot be accomplished if the victim is killed—the larva will die from hunger. If the number of the larva is disproportional to the size of the body, the larva will also die from malnutrition. Equality operates the same way—equality needs inequality to exist and reproduce. The Russian socialists (communists) did not follow the script of Nature and just killed their victim—the fat body of capitalism. And the larva of equality died soon, as well.

"They made a mistake in their quest for equality," cry other brands of socialists, progressives, community organizers and others proponents of equality in the US and Europe. "We will correct this strategic mistake."

Now, they do not want to kill a fat body of free-market capitalism; they need inequality for their socialist larva (Unions, ACORNs, environmentalists, global-warming activists, anti-globalists, global altruists, anti-corporatists, feminists, peaceniks and others) to feed on it. But the larva will kill capitalism unintentionally due to insatiable appetite, which is disproportional to the size of the victim's body. In both cases, the end is the same: equality will bring poverty and misery.

No wonder, since the 1990s, most of the socialist parties in the world turned to the free-market capitalist system for solutions, burying the socialist ideals of equality in so-called mixed economy. Does this make them semi-socialists or semi-capitalists? The bankrupted Marxist's-Leninist's dogma of planned, state socialism was rejected almost everywhere, even in Russia—the birthplace of the dogma. Their call is loud and clear, but the socialists in the US have a hearing problem, I guess.

All Rise! The Nature's Court is in Session! Equality vs. Reality!

In the eyes of Nature, economic equality is an absurdity, but it is not evident to most people until it is too late: until all resources are equally and irreversibly redistributed between all like in the former USSR.

Therefore, let's resort to an allegory to illustrate this point clearly. Let's imagine that the proponents of Equality are complaining about inequality in distribution of the solar energy around the globe. They present a seemingly valid and convincing case in favor of equality in the Circuit Court of … Nature.

All rise! The Nature's Court is in Session! Honorable Judge Nature is presiding! Equality vs. Reality!

"Your Honor, we are genuinely concerned about poor polar bears freezing to death at -89°C on the vicious South Pole and about poor camels boiling alive in the deserts at +56°C on the scorching Equator. This unfair practice exists even when some privileged creatures live in comfortable climate (at +25°C). We want fair energy redistribution around the globe; we want to change the climate so that all creatures live at equal temperature and in comfortable climate everywhere.

"Will everyone feel comfortable if planet temperature is equalized?" Judge Nature asks.

"Absolutely, Your Honor, they will if the existing inequality is eliminated. We have a theory of socio-economic justice which predicts just that."

"But the opponents assert that this solar energy inequality is the result of a spherical shape of the planet Earth and the inclination of its axis," the Judge objects. "Also, polar bears and camels can migrate into a milder climate if they wish."

"Those are the excuses to justify such blatant inequality, your Honor."

"Did you consider all the consequences?" the Judge warns.

"Yes, your Honor, we did. Our theory predicts sunny and comfortable climate for everyone."

"Fine! Do it at your peril, but I take a disclaimer," Judge Nature says. Nature has never been against those taking risk as long as it goes with taking responsibility.

And the proponents of Equality did it against Nature's warning. How? We can only guess. Of course, the "unlimited" power of a human mind cannot warm the North and air condition the deserts. But nuclear flattening of the Earth sphere into a pancake can certainly do it and more in line with a human nature.

Anyway, the community organizers collected all the solar energy and spread it equally around the globe. Now, every spot on the planet Pancake (formerly Earth) is receiving the same amount of solar energy. And it works. No freezing or boiling to death temperatures any more.

But what the hell is that? The land temperature around the globe[1] is equalized at chilling...8.5°C (47.3°F).

"This is not what we had in mind," the hard-core proponents of equality are scratching their heads. "We meant equal and comfortable temperatures everywhere."

The unforeseen (typical for an "unlimited" human mind) consequences of the forced climate change did not keep Man waiting for long. Since the temperature is equal, there is no air movement and no wind; low temperature means little evaporation and little rain; not enough solar energy and rain mean little food is produced. Other catastrophes follow one after another—rising of the ocean level from thawing of polar ice caps; flooding of costal lands; lack of oxygen in the atmosphere; drying out of the soil; and eventually…famine.

The simple truth is that there is not enough solar energy to make every place *equally comfortable* for living on Earth. Those who promise both equal and comfortable climate for all are living in a comfortable climate or lying.

Economic Equality has the same inherent and chronic problem: *there are not enough resources to make both equal and comfortable living for everyone on the planet Earth.*

Equality can make everyone only *equally* miserable and hungry. The allegories describing the removal of hills and the forced climate change, although exaggerated, illustrate the absurdity of the concept of Equality.

No wonder, there is no trace of equality in Nature—the idea was born by and, like a parasite, can live only in a human mind of impractical intellectuals. It defies human nature and is far from reality.

Equality means that some people have a *"free lunch and a free ride."* But Nature has no budget for such luxury. Equality contradicts Nature; it insults and deceives human nature and intelligence.

Therefore, Equality as a concept and practice are doomed to failure sooner or later like the grandiose bloody human equality experiments in the former USSR and other socialist countries.

Does Equality Keep Its Promises?

The promises of Equality are very appealing: better life; abundance instead of misery; spirituality instead of envy and greed; altruism instead of egoism; and freedom to do what you like. But does Equality keep these promises?

No, it does not! I testify to that as a witness who lived in the land of Equality for more than 40 years. Equality comes with a heavy price for everyone. But this price is never disclosed to the poor little polar bears and camels in the contract offered by the proponents of Equality.

The contract does not spell out that the leveling of the playing field means that the rivers would stop running and would turn into swamps. The contract does not spell out that the equal distribution of energy means that the masses of air and water vapor would stop moving around; would stop aerating and moisturizing the planet; that the currents would stop flowing and spreading nutrients and oxygen around the oceans and atmosphere.

What the contract implies is that everyone will be equally rich. And we buy this stereotype picture about Equality. But how about this picture—everyone is equally poor? Is this still Equality? Yes, it is equality, but on the lowest (poverty) level. So, there is more than one concept of Equality. When everyone is equally rich or equally poor, those are just two opposite extremes of Equality.

So far, Man was very "successful" at reaching equality on the poverty level. Remember equal solar energy distribution on the planet Pancake? Everyone had to live at 8.5°C (47.3°F) all year long—a good recipe for famine. The experience of the socialist states proved it over and over again. Almost entire population of the USSR used to live *equally* below the poverty level (by the US standards); they lived in misery *equally* deprived of every necessity.

But is it possible to reach equality on the highest level? That is what every proponent of Equality silently implies and sells. Do you know any historical example of a society where everyone was rich? It is called Utopia. There are not enough resources on a small planet like Earth to make every one rich.

What about intermediate levels of Equality? This is like the entire country, or the world consists of the middle class? Can you imagine a fantastic society like that? Every homeless, welfare recipient or resident of Palm Beach, Florida belongs to the middle class and earns the same.

This is Utopia too. There are not enough resources to make everyone the middle class either. Just look at the equal distribution of solar energy around the globe and the resulting average global temperature of $8.5^{\circ}C$! Does it look like a comfortable temperature or the one at the mid of a household thermometer scale? A similar, equal global income distribution will not make all people the middle class—not even close; it would rather make them all poor as will be proven later.

Isn't that ironic that the only country that came close to the ideals of the intermediate level of Equality is the United States of America, the capitalist free-market society, which is based...on shameless inequality.

So, the only equality the socialists can offer to a prosperity-longing human society is the equality on the poverty level as in the USSR. It is like the notorious apple offered by the Witch to the naive Snow White: red and appetizing outside; dark and poisonous inside. Let's dissect the equality apple and look what is inside of it.

ANATOMY OF EQUALITY

Equality vs. Free-Market Economy

I am sitting on the bench outside of a jewelry store on a crooked, crowded street of a small Caribbean island waiting for my wife. She disappeared inside the store with other tourists arrived on our cruise liner, and I feel this is for long this time. A man in his 50's is sitting next to me as bored as I am, apparently in the same hopeless situation.

"Brothers in distress," I say trying to strike a conversation to kill time.

"A very true observation," the man is laughing. "My name is Otto, Otto Gross from Germany." We shake hands, and I introduce myself. It turned out that we both work as engineers. We talk a little bit about our profession, the ship and vacation. Then, Otto looks around and says:

"I am thinking about those poor people that have to sell all these trifles and contra fits to the rich tourists to make a living. When I see something like that and compare it with our luxury life, I feel nothing but guilt and compassion for those less fortunate people. I have a nice house in the suburb; attached garage with two cars in it; a good-paying job and more. They have nothing."

"Do you feel personally responsible for their bad fortune?" I ask.

"No, I don't, but we all are, I guess."

"Will you feel better if everyone has to sell trifles for a living too?"

"God forbid, of course not. But I believe they should live as comfortable as we and our children do."

"But how can we do this?" I ask with poorly disguised phony naivety.

"I think that all of us, especially the rich, should sacrifice more to make it happen. Then, there would be no guilt and envy, and every one would be happy."

"Hey, here is my princess coming out!" Otto says introducing me to his wife. We shake hands, and they leave in a hurry: there are so many stores to visit in a couple of hours.

I am sitting on the bench and thinking about the brief conversation. Is Otto an idealistic dreamer or he is a conscious proponent of economic Equality? Is this ignorance or naivety to think this way in the early 80s of the 20th century as if the US and USSR do not exist?

I got the answers very soon when I found myself on another bench next to Otto outside of another store. We laugh at such coincidence, and the conversation interrupted earlier continues. But this time I decide to turn it into a debate.

"So, you are advocating economic equality, aren't you?" I am trying to provoke Otto to open up more.

"Yes, I am. And I see that a lot of progress has already been made in this respect, in the US and especially in Europe."

"Then, can you clarify for me the principle of economic equality using the following hypothetical situation? Let's assume, that Paul and Peter work for the same employer as engineers of equal qualification. Paul earns $2,400/month working 8 hours a day, while Peter by some reasons works only 4 hours a day and earns $1,200/month. Both are compensated equally at the same hourly rates.

The reasons why Pete is working less than Paul could be slow economy; employer thinks that Pete is less productive; Pete hates his work; he does not care about money that much; he drinks; he is lazy; he needs some leisure time; you name it.

Is an hourly rate is a genuine criterion of fairness and equality? Since both Paul and Pete are paid equal hourly rates, this is g*enuine economic equality*—equal pay for equal work. It offers them an equal opportunity to earn, not equal earning. Paul earns more because he works more hours than Pete."

"Sorry, but I have to disagree," Otto says. "I think that a better criterion of fairness and economic equality is how much everyone earns. The mere fact that Paul is allowed to earn more is unfair; it creates inequality. *Economic equality* can be reached when both of them earn equally."

"But your concept of economic equality is, in fact, the *reward equality* (equal reward for unequal work)," I object. "It cares only about equal rewards, but it does take into account the contributions, the fact that Paul works more."

"It does not matter that Paul works more; it does not change the principle. It is still unfair to have more," Otto insists.

"...Boys, are you still debating?" Otto's wife comes out carrying a bunch of packages. The conversation is interrupted again and for good this time.

There was nothing to debate. It is perfectly clear that I am a strong proponent of a free-market capitalist economic system based on inequality, while Otto is a strong proponent of a socialist economic system based on equality and fairness. And there is nothing I can do to change Otto's mind as long as he has a nice house in the suburb; attached garage with two cars in it; a good-paying job and more.

Equality vs. Socialist Economy

Although Otto left, I continue to debate him in my mind. *Fairness* is an attack weapon in Otto's lexicon and a pain killer for his *Guilt*. But when *Fairness* wakes up, its friend *Envy* wakes up too. Both will advise Pete to demand an equal reward regardless of Paul's greater contribution. The reward equality is a solid foundation of any socialist economic system.

Let's assume that socialists destroyed a free-market economy (as they always do) and delivered economic Equality. Now, Paul and Pete have to work equal number of hours a day and receive equal salaries, both the hours and the salary being determined by the state. Now, the socialists proclaim they achieved genuine equality—equal reward for equal work.

But why don't I hear any cheers, Otto? It is because there are two main problems. The first one is meager salaries; a kid at a free-market McDonalds used to earn much more. As I said, the inherent problem with Equality is that there are not enough resources on the planet Earth to make everyone to live as comfortable as you do, Otto. Now, Paul and Pete "enjoy" equality, but below the poverty level.

I am not joking about the salaries, Otto. In 1979 when I came to the US, average monthly salaries of an engineer in the USSR and the US were about 120 rubles vs. $2,000. A new car at that time in the USSR (5-8 years waiting list) and the US cost about 6,000 rubles (50 months of work) vs. $6,000 (3 months of work).

Do you feel the difference, Otto? This is 101 of Equality. Everyone must be aware of the misery that follows socialism, especially those who are eaten by guilt for being well-to-do.

But wait! There is even more serious problem than salaries. While hard-working Paul works harder and produces more than lazy Peter does (because Nature said so), the socialist economy forbids Paul to earn more no matter how hard he tries and how big his contribution is. This is one of the main functions of a socialist state to keep the disparity in income to a minimum— the core principle of socialism that defies Nature.

This absurd principle was the reality of everyday life in the USSR. Here is my personal story. Andrew and William were two engineers working in my laboratory. Andrew was a shirker, a drunkard and an unproductive bum, while William was extremely hard-working, creative and could handle any assignment. I could not cut Andrew's salary or give William a bigger raise he deserved—both salaries were set up by the state to prevent the disparity (inequality). I could not fire Andrew either – full employment was a law. To get rid of Andrew, I had to find an equal replacement job for him first, which I did. What a country! Cheers to the forced full employment and equality!

This was not a genuine equality—equal reward for equal work. This was the reward equality—equal reward for unequal work or unequal reward for equal work; take your pick, Otto. And here is my last word, Otto:

"Socialist Equality is a concealed form of Inequality!"

Equality: Gifted vs. Ordinary People

Do you need an illustration of the socialist inequality, Otto? Just compare how the two economic systems treat people deserving higher rewards for their talents and extraordinary contribution to the society.

Every human society produces talented people—a few geniuses and a small group of gifted individuals. The rest are average people because Nature said so. But those few talented people make disproportionate contributions to the society. Think about people who caused radical changes in science, technology and medicine; and those who are able to put their discovery and innovations to practice. Due to enormous contributions of this small minority, the majority of average people enjoys more prosperity and achieves it sooner than they would have without those few. Read Nature's lips: *the prosperity of average people depends on how the talented people are rewarded by the society.*

A free-market economy, the land of repugnant inequality, is based on rewards and contributions. The talents contribute more and are rewarded more, while average people contribute less and are rewarded less. In many cases, contribution of talented people is not possible to quantify with dollars. It can be valued only by our imagination. In this respect, the reward-to-contribution ratio (R/C) may be a qualitative criterion of fairness and equality (similar to a quantitative hourly rate).

For example, Bill Gates earned billions. What a blatant inequality! But this is a testimony of how a capitalist society cherishes talented people. Despite his enormous reward, he made an incalculable contribution to the society raising prosperity of the entire humanity. If his reward (in $ billions) had been divided by his enormous contribution (in $ billions), then his R/C might have been less than that of average people whose relative contribution is close to zero.

The same principle is universally applied to all gifted people, inventors, businessmen, entrepreneurs, financiers, CEOs, musicians, writers, artists and others. Their contributions are usually much greater than their rewards. After all, the capitalist's inequality may be closer to genuine equality and fairness than the reward equality offered by the socialist system.

In contrast, in the USSR, talented people were appallingly mistreated. It is hard to believe, but world-class scientists whose discoveries revolutionized the technology; ingenious inventors whose inventions were worth millions; outstanding brain surgeons; world-renown artists, musicians or athletes—all of them were rewarded much less than they deserved.

Here is the real story about musicians. In the late 70s, the Leningrad Philharmonic Orchestra was one of the world's most famous symphony orchestra under outstanding conductor Yevgeny Mravinsky. The orchestra was comprised of the world's most talented musicians. Contrary to other citizens, these musicians were allowed to tour the world: they were bringing large amounts of so needed currency to the starving socialist state. But the musicians received only about $20 a day (10% of what they earned) for their unforgettable performances. The musicians had to take food (sausages, canned products, etc) on each tour hiding it in their musical instruments from the KGB chaperons to save every penny. The legendary violinist David Oistrakh was allowed to keep only $250 for his performance. At the same time, average and less talented musicians in the West received thousands! Welcome to the socialist economic equality!

The rewards the talented people received in the USSR were negligible, but the contributions were enormous. Thus, their R/C was close to zero. In other words, talented slaves were savagely abused and exploited by the socialist, egalitarian system. Some of them were working just for food in secret organizations (urban labor camps in the communist GULAG system) specially organized for imprisoned people of unique skills and talents.

One of those talented people locked up there was Andrei Tupolev, a famous aircraft designer who created numerous military aircraft for the Soviet air force and commercial aviation. Another was Sergei Korolev, a famous rocket scientist who created and launched the first Sputnik on the orbit around the Earth and later built many spacecrafts. There were many others who were transferred from the horrible concentration camps in Siberia to work in such secret organizations-prisons just for food.

In other words, the talented people were robbed by the socialist economic system for the sake of Equality. As a result, there were little incentives to make as many contributions to the society as the talented people potentially could. But without incentives, there was universal poverty in the USSR instead of prosperity!

Can Talented Slaves Create?

"So what?" you may say. "Talented slaves can create too." That's true! Talented slaves can create and produce...out of hunger or out of fear for their lives. But when people are brutally forced or threatened to do so, very few are capable to open their mind to the fullest extent of their abilities due to lack of enthusiasm and burden of stress—this is a natural limitation of a human character. Too bad because the pace of progress in modern science and technology depends not only on the contributions of a few geniuses, but on enthusiasm and the fullest contribution of all talented people and average people, as well.

Creativity and risk taking are two legs, on which science, technology and industry are running in a free capitalist society. Voluntary creativity flourishes in a free society and free-market economy. In fact, one of the most prominent inborn traits of a human nature has always been the spirit of entrepreneurship. Voluntary creativity and risk taking are natural for free people because they are motivated by incentives—the expectation of adequate rewards. Creativity is like a free bird; it develops emotional problems in a cage.

"Not true," cry socialists. "People do not need "bourgeois" material incentives to create and produce. There are incentives that are much more appealing to a human nature, namely altruistic incentives—to live for and serve others."

And all people in the USSR were forced to live and create for others altruistically without material incentives. Such blatant abuse of a human nature created a lack of enthusiasm and the vacuum was filled with...fear, which is a poor surrogate for enthusiasm.

Fear was one of the main drags for creativity in the USSR; fear of failure, which meant lost jobs, exile, imprisonment or even death. The failure to detonate the Soviet atomic bomb during the first test in August 1949 would have meant death sentences for all developers of the bomb. Therefore, the risk taking was the last resort for everyone; it was never worth of limited rewards received by geniuses (a free car or an apartment) or talented people (diplomas, badges or small bonuses). This is one of the main reasons why the socialist economy without incentives could not run or walk—it was limping on both legs.

"Not true," cry socialists again. "The planned, state-run socialist economy thrived in the USSR. Look at their impressive achievements in science and technology—space program; theoretical science; aircraft industry; nuclear technology; astronomy; and other programs."

Let's see if this is true, point by point. The inferiority of the socialist economy, science, technology and industry was clearly revealed in the article "The Limits of Soviet Technology" by Louis Lavoie, a military systems analyst at the Defense Systems Division of Honeywell, Inc. The article was published just several years before the collapse of the Soviet Union (November/December 1985 issue of the Technology Review edited by the Massachusetts Institute of Technology).

Let's start with the space program, the pride of the Soviets. In the early 1960s, the USSR had initial superiority in the space technology (Sputnik, animal and then man in space, etc.). But it was gained largely due to prohibitively enormous resources invested in this field (at the expense of many other technologies), while absolute secrecy gave the Soviets a tremendous head start. However, once it became an open race, it took the US less than a decade to leave the USSR far behind in the space exploration. For example, from 1960 to 1985, the USSR made 5 times more space launches than the US. But by the end of this period, only 5% of the Soviet satellites were still functioning due to poor reliability in comparison with 18% of the US satellites. The Soviet scientists launched numerous satellites in space, but they failed to detect one of the Earth's most prominent features, the Van Allen radiation belts—the result of poor instrumentation. The belt was easily detected by the early US satellites. Other examples of the US superiority are well known—moon exploration, space shuttles, international space station, and others.

Achievements in the Soviet basic science were also less significant than they appeared. From 1901 (when the Nobel Prize was established) and to the mid 1980s, the US scientists have won 132 prices, while the USSR—only...8! Such miserable results were achieved despite the fact that the best talents were recruited into the field (including Nobel Prize winners Pyotr Kapitsa, Nikolai Basov and Lev Landau) and despite an army of scientists and engineers in the supporting roles (for curious, more than 1 million). Here is another example. The "phase-stability" principle (used to accelerate subatomic particles) was discovered by the Soviet physicist Vladimir Veksler. However, none of the hundreds of elementary particles found by the mid 1980s was discovered by the Soviet scientists despite the existence of one of the world's largest proton synchrotron at Protvino near Moscow and other Soviet facilities.

The inferiority of the Soviet aircraft industry was evident to everyone. The Soviets could not sell their commercial aircrafts even to the Third World airlines, even at a half price of comparable US jets. Frequent air disasters, even at the international air shows speak volume about their reliability. The inferiority of the Soviet military aircraft was repeatedly demonstrated in wars between air forces of Israel and its Arab neighbors flying Soviet-made MIGs.

The backwardness of the Soviet nuclear technology had been a common knowledge, from the moment when the secrets of the atomic bomb were stolen from the US and to the time of the Chernobyl nuclear disaster.

The world's largest Soviet telescope with a 6-m diameter single mirror turned out to be useless for advanced astronomical work due to inferior mirror design and poor image quality. But it was used for PR purposes on an astronomical scale as many other Soviet achievements.

The backwardness of the Soviets in computers, genetics and other fundamental scientific disciplines was well-known facts and was not accidental also.

Do you need more facts and examples? There are too many to bring them all up. Despite of all their apparent achievements, the USSR was a backward country of the Third World that fueled its development by the infusion of the advanced Western technologies and innovations through illegal acquisition, patent infringement or theft. These facts were common knowledge in the USSR, in the US and everywhere else.

For example, Xerox copying even a single sheet of paper regardless of its content at my place of work (or any other working places in the USSR) required special permission from plant KGB representative and plant management. But when I went to work for the defense industry in the US, I was shocked by the volume of information about numerous military and commercial innovations published in free scientific and technical literature. This information would be considered of extremely classified nature in the USSR.

"Aren't you afraid to tip the Soviets?" I asked one of the military analysts once.

"Not really," he replied. "They are too backward to copy correctly the avalanche of these innovations and too slow to bring them to the field fast enough. When they do, these technologies are already obsolete. On the other hand, free transfer of information has always been a powerful technology accelerator in a free and open society."

So, can the forced equality instigated by fear combined with coerced altruism replace incentives? Nope! To expect the fullest creative contribution from people working without incentives is to go against a human nature. Therefore, science and technology in an egalitarian, socialist society has always been stagnating and lagging far behind in direct competition with the creative free-market capitalist world!

This is the main reason why capitalism has to be destroyed first for socialism to exist. As the revolutionary hymn of the Socialist Internationale reads (in Russian translation): "We will destroy this world of violence down to the foundations *and then* we will build our new world." As the history confirmed, the socialists are extremely good in destroying rather than building.

Is Equality a Myth?

Equality has never been in existence at anytime, anywhere in the world. There is only inequality, the capitalist or the socialist inequalities.

In a free-market economy, inequality is openly and honestly displayed. You are rewarded more than others if you contribute more. If your talent or work ethics has no limits, your reward has no limits too. This principle was learned and borrowed from Nature, not born in a human mind. It follows the law of Nature: "The early bird gets the worm." It is fairer and closer to genuine equality than it is usually portrayed in liberal media.

In a socialist economy, inequality is out of sight or is cowardly disguised as equality. Individuals are rewarded equally regardless of their contribution. (Reward is on display; contribution is not). The state decides how much everyone should earn. Your reward is the same no matter how productive, hard-working and inventive you are. This absurd principle is a product of a human mind, not Nature. The late bird will never get any worm in Nature. Such bird cannot survive; it will starve to death. What would have happened if a free give-away of worms had existed in Nature? Shortage of worms! Birds would lose their worm-getting skills and then would die out.

The reward equality is equal reward for not equal contribution. Such blatant inequality I saw every day living in the former USSR. The rewards of the most talented, capable and dedicated people were not much different than that of the mediocre, idle and lazy ones. Also, it was incomparable with your standard of living, Otto.

Well, the intentions might be good, but the reality was ugly—nobody worked hard. Why work hard? A full employment was guaranteed by law and enforced regardless of necessity. As we used to joke: "The best wrestlers in the world are the Soviet workers: they wrestle with hunger before lunch and with doziness—for the rest of the working day." It is absurdity, isn't it? Yes, *but in the eyes of a socialist, a good intention is a substitute for reality and economics.*

The economic system that is bent on good intentions of eradicating the unemployment at any cost is an artificial system that could not survive for long. For example, due to limited capabilities, the shipyard where I worked could build trawlers for fishing only close to shores. But fishermen cried out for years that there was no fish left there; they needed the open-sea ships. Instead of shutting the damn place down, the state forced us to build and fishermen to buy more and more worthless ships every year.

Good intentions? Well, there was no unemployment in the Land of Equality! As the only employer, the socialist state could create any number of jobs. As we joked: "One guy digs a pit, while another fills it in at the same time; both are occupied and paid equally by the state. This comic symbol of the full-employment socialism was not far from reality.

Here is another absurdity! Nikita Khrushchev fell in love with corn during his visit to the US in 1959. Very soon, Soviet collective farms were forced to grow corn everywhere (except tundra) at the expense of more profitable traditional crops. There was no incentive for people to do that. The result was food shortages. It is another absurdity, isn't it? Yes, *the socialist, centralized, planned economy devoid of incentives is a theater of absurd.*

Conclusions: the capitalist economic system based on inequality and incentives is closer to equality and fairness than the socialist economic system. And visa versa. The socialist economic system based on reward equality and good intentions harbors inequality and injustice. The road to Equality is a vicious circle paved by good intentions, which leads from prosperity to poverty.

Why does Equality always lead to disastrous results? This is because *Equality is just a myth!* It does not exist in Nature, and it does not exist in an egalitarian society, as well. Here is the roadmap to socialist economic Equality:

(Capitalist inequality + Prosperity) → *Envy* → *Socialist equality* → *(Inequality + Poverty).*

"The inherent vice of capitalism is an unequal sharing of blessings; the inherent vice of socialism is an equal sharing of misery."
Winston Churchill.

SHAKE DOWN THE RICH

Poverty or Poverty Game?

Of course, you may say that the demolition of hills and the solar energy redistribution are just allegories and fantasies. Excuse me! Most of people know or heard someone who calls for the destruction of capitalism and wealth redistribution. The motive is "noble"—to achieve economic equality and social justice, here in the US or abroad.

Poverty! This is an immensely powerful and hated image in the eyes of a well-fed, well-dressed and well-sheltered American liberal. And when the gross inequality in income distribution and poverty are exposed, they demand income equality without thinking about the consequences for themselves.

Who lives in poverty in the US? According to the US Census Bureau Report[2], people live in poverty when their income is below a threshold that depends on family size and number of children. The threshold is set by the US Government, which, I would say, is open for subjective interpretation. In fact, the Census Bureau Report[2] (Appendix B) determined that the 2008 minimum threshold for a household (1 person in household, no children) was *$11,201,* and maximum threshold for a multi-person family was...*$47,915.*

How many of 301 million Americans did live in poverty in 2008, in the midst of the recession? The Census Bureau[2] says 39.8 million or 13.2% (compare with 22% and 15% in 1959 and 1980 recessions, respectively). However, most of them lived in poverty only temporarily, including those who were short-term unemployed. "Chronic" poverty is relatively uncommon, as Census Bureau clarifies, with only 1.8% living in poverty for 48 months or longer[2].

When I and my family came to the US virtually penniless, we were euphoric about this wealthy, generous and compassionate country. Once, I was invited by a colleague of mine for a dinner. As usual, the topic at the table among his liberal, affluent friends was about the poor.

"How do you like this country? I was asked.

"What a country!" I replied. "I've never seen so many wealthy, generous and compassionate people."

But the guests snubbed me right away: "There are so many poor people here too. Have you ever seen them in the Government-subsidized apartments, living in poverty?"

"Yes, I have. In fact, my parents are living there now. As everyone there, they have a small, one-bedroom, air-conditioned and heated apartment; a refrigerator; free health care; SSI check, food stamps and energy assistance from the Government. They never lived that well in their entire life, while working back home. Their income is greater than my salary of an engineer back in the USSR, for God's sake!"

"But most of them are hungry; they had to save on food in order to buy a TV, a microwave, phones, cameras and other necessary stuff. There are so many hungry people around us!"

"So, why many of those hungry people are fat?" I asked naively.

"You probably don't know anything about hunger. The research shows that they are fat because they have to eat wrong food at McDonalds! "

What can I say? When a liberal paints a picture of how the poor live in the US, hunger is the predominant color in that picture. Well-fed Americans cannot imagine, understand and stomach a horrible image of hunger. This image is the best tool in the hands of shrewd operators to manipulate naïve, satiated people into buying that picture.

Hunger! Oh, I do know about hunger painfully well. I starved as a child during the war and almost died from hunger. My relatives were starving in Leningrad during the German blockade. Academia does not define what hunger is; your stomach does.

Hunger is when you are chewing a piece of stinking black tar found on railway tracks to dull the pain in your stomach. Hunger is when you are splitting your daily ration (a palm-size slice of bread mixed with wooden sawdust) in three pieces to deceive your stomach. Hunger is when your spine says hello to your stomach. When you are fat and eating hamburgers in a restaurant, this is not hunger. This is something else.

When an affluent American is told about "less fortunate" people, the implication is that some people are "more fortunate" because they won a lottery; not because they are more talented and work harder than others; more creative, inventive and venturous. Strange it may seem, but most of heart-bleeding liberals are more fortunate themselves and some are outright filthy rich. Being infected and corroded by gilt, they feel good by fighting for noble causes of economic equality and fairness, while enjoying living in their big houses in affluent suburbs.

But watch what you wish for. This "feel-good" game is not what you think. It is a dangerous ride on a one-way, high-speed bullet train. When you board it, the doors (bars) are slammed shut behind you by a shrewd train operator. The train does not stop, and you cannot get off until it brings you straight to a destination called "Equality."

Let's make an imaginable trip on this bullet train. The route and schedule are graciously provided by the shrewd socialist operators from my old country. Let's assume that, in 2005, we have passed the first couple of stations of this trip. The income redistribution has already taken place: a good chunk of income of the rich has already been expropriated for the public good.

So, how much has already been expropriated so far in the US? Just look up the reports[3] issued by the US Congressional Budget Office (CBO). Here, the incomes of the filthy rich and other fat cats for a prosperous year 2005 are posted. I assembled these pre-tax and after-tax data in the tables below along with my calculations (the CBO data are printed in bold).

2005 US PRETAX INCOME

Top income categ. (%)	No of house-holds (mil)	Average income/ h/hold ($)	Tot income (all h/holds) ($ bil)	(%)	US popu-lation (mil)	Average income/ person ($)
All	**114.5**	**84,800**	**9,709**	**100.0**	**301**	32,258
Top 10	**11.7**	**339,100**	3,967	**40.9**		
Top 5	**5.8**	**520,200**	3,017	**31.1**		
Top 1	**1.1**	**1,558,500**	1,714	**18.1**		

2005 US AFTERTAX INCOME

Top income categ. (%)	No of house-holds (mil)	Average income/ h/hold ($)	Tot income (all h/holds) ($ bil)	(%)	Total taxes (all h/holds) ($ bil)	(%)	Equal redistrib/ person* ($)
All	**114.5**	**67,400**	**7,717**	**100.0**	**1,992**	**100.0**	
Top 10	**11.7**	**246,300**	2,881	**37.4**	1,085	**27.4**	9,574
Top 5	**5.8**	**369,800**	2,144	**27.8**	872	**28.9**	7,126
Top 1	**1.1**	**1,071,500**	1,178	**15.6**	535	**31.2**	3,916

Note* – This is how much every person would have received if after-tax income of the rich had been expropriated and equally redistributed among the US population in 2005.

I used the term "expropriation" (popular in Marxist's terminology) intentionally. By definition, the term means to take away property or money belonging to somebody, either legally for public good or illegally by theft or fraud. Both tactics are equally popular. But contrary to the USSR, the main tool of expropriation in the US is not a gun, but taxes and inflation. It is a pure coincidence, of course, that Vladimir Lenin, the founder of the USSR, once said: *"The way to crush bourgeoisie is to grind them between the millstones of taxation and inflation."* It is a sinister prediction for the socialists in the US and a glorious roadmap for them to follow!

The table above shows that there were 1.1 million of the rich households in 2005? They are in the top 1% by income distribution, but their share is 18% ($1.7 trillion) of total income earned by all ($9.7 trillion). This 1% paid 31% of all taxes—a half a trillion dollars! Surprise! We were told that the rich did not pay taxes or did not pay enough—financial tricks, loopholes, you know. Shame! Those high taxes paid by the rich are needed to help the poor.

However, if the $535 billion in taxes the rich paid had been distributed among 37 million[2] of the poor people living in poverty in 2005, every poor person would have collected up to...$14,460! Each household of four would have collected almost $57,838! So, why are 40 million poor people still living in poverty in 2008? Where did those taxes go? As long as we have the poor, the class struggle continues.

Shake down the Rich: How much Every One would Get?

And the bullet train is rushing on to its final destination Equality. Now, we are approaching the next station and we hear the same voices again: "the rich do not pay their fair share."

The implication is that income of the rich does not belong to them; it was directly deposited in the imaginable *National Equality Bank*. Then, the income was somehow fraudulently distributed, the poor being robbed from their lawful, fair share by the rich.

Who are those rich people the proponents of equality hate so much? They are those who own corporations and banks; big investors, venture capitalists, the people who create and finance industries, factories and shopping malls; and eventually create jobs. What are they those rich people? They are what we are not.

They are more entrepreneurial than any of us. (By Forbes' 2010 list, 7 of 10 top billionaires were self-made, and only three are not, but multiplied their wealth).

They have better vision of the future trends than all of us. (Look at Bill Gates, Microsoft; Sergey Brin and Larry Page, Google; or Lawrence Elliot, Oracle).

They are willing to take more risk with their future and investments than most of us. (Bill Gates dropped out of Harvard to pursue his dream; Jeff Bezos left his Wall Street executive job to start Amazon).

They have more patience and fortitude than most of us; and they are willing to endure more hardship in pursuit of success. Jeff Bezos started Amazon company in his garage and was struggling for 7 years (due to the disillusionment caused by the dotcom crash) until people were ready to shop online.

They are more frugal and disciplined in saving; and they are watching the bottom line more carefully than any of us. (Warren Buffett, Berkshire Hathaway is an example).

There are millions of those who are investing fearlessly and wisely; building industries; hiring people; having more talents and working harder than most of us.

But the perception is quite the opposite, thanks to our progressive media! The notion is that the rich are parasites; that their wealth is inherited or amassed dishonestly at the expense not only the poor, but everyone. Therefore, heavier taxes on the rich are warranted and are considered today to help not only the poor, but the middle class (the rest of us), as well. This slogan is appealing to everyone today, not only to the poor.

So, what will happen when the bullet train reaches the next station? At the next station, *all* after-tax income of the rich (top 1%) will be expropriated and redistributed equally among all of us. Good! What a historic moment predicted by Marx! Now, the problem of the poor will be solved. So, how much would everyone get? (See the CBO table above).

O-o-ops, only *$3,916* per person! Is that all? For most of us, it is not enough even to pay off our credit card debts. But before we boarded the train, the shrewd operators told us that, by expropriating the rich, we would be able to eliminate poverty! What a disappointment! Did they make a mistake or lie? Well, never mind; they will fix the mistake at the next station. And the bullet train is rolling on, and the class struggle is continuing.

At the next passing station, we hear demands to shake down the larger group of the wealthy people, the top 5% (all those CEO's of corporations and banks; entrepreneurs who take risks; those who make the business engine running; those who employ people and give them paychecks and benefits, you know). Now, everyone would receive additional *$3,210*!

Shoot! It is still not enough! Again, we hear about the poor and poverty. Who is next to be axed? Oh, the top 10%! They are well-to-do people, who own middle and small businesses; who hire most of the workers. Now, everyone would become richer by another *$2,448*!

Will all 13% of the poor be snatched out of poverty, now? Wishful thinking! We need poor. Will those 10% of the rich, wealthy and well-to-do people declare no income and be qualified as poor living in poverty? No, they will not do that. But they will close their bankrupted businesses. Of course, they will. Will they lay off people? Yes, they will. Will they leave the US? You bet. Who will the Government expropriate from and who will they ask to help the poor the next year?

Will they ask us? No, we were duped! Stop the train, I want to get off...Too late—the bullet train is running non-stop. Again, we hear the same annoying voices that the poor are still far from getting their fair share. Next in line will be the top 25%; then everyone who earns above and then below the average.

And, eventually, the bullet train reaches its destination Equality. All assets and incomes will be ceased from everyone. The Government will become one monster corporation and will pay every one equal salary. It will also take care of all your needs, your needs being determined by the Government too. If you want to know what a humanitarian catastrophe follows, just read the history of the Bolshevik's socialist revolution in Russia in 1917. They did exactly that—they killed the rich and then...

You still don't believe that our country is moving toward socialism, one legislative act at a time. Is an act such as "stimulus package" leads us there? Let's trace it to the socialist roots. Does it create government's jobs, at the expense of private sector's jobs? Of course! Can you become rich on a government's payroll? Absolutely not! So, the "stimulus" is the road to economic equality—a socialist ideal, which can be achieved when most of jobs are the government's jobs.

Eliminate the rich! What a tempting idea contemplated again today—a "natural" instinct of a socialist. But is it natural? In his book Shark Life, the bestselling author of Jaws Peter Benchley described seaside villagers living in harmony with Nature and respecting the rules of Life. And Nature loves them back—they were making a decent living catching plenty of lobsters and fish year after year.

One day the villagers discovered that all the sharks, big and small, were lying dead on the sea bottom. The sharks were mutilated by Man for their valuable possession—fins. Well, shark-fin soup is a very expensive delicacy.

Some people were alarmed about the disappearance of sharks. But most of them did not worry too much. Well, shark is a vicious, dangerous and insatiable predator that steals fish from poor fishermen and is an enemy of Man. But Nature disagreed and gave Man an unforgettable lesson.

A shark is at the top of the food chain—the role given it by Nature. The sharks preyed on octopuses and when the sharks disappeared, the octopuses overran the reef. Since lobster is their favorite food, the lobster's population suddenly crashed. But this is not all. In absence of sharks preying upon the sea lion colony nearby, the sea lion's population exploded too. Now, the fish population was devastated by the sea lions also.

Disappearance of lobsters and fish affected everyone—the mates who worked on the boats; the fishermen who caught lobster and fish; the wholesalers on the dock who bought, processed and packed them; the truckers who took them to the stores and restaurants; people who worked and served there; and many others. Like ripples spreading from a stone dropped in a pond, more and more people were hit by the disaster. They were loosing boats and businesses, homes and cars and, eventually, their livelihood until the entire area was devastated and deserted. Thus, Nature turned the sea catastrophe caused by arrogant, ignorant Man into Man's catastrophe.

...Isn't that what socialists try to do? Like sharks eliminated for their fins, the rich and the prosperous are eliminated for their wealth. But the rich—those vicious, dangerous and insatiable predators that steal from the poor— are, in a way, at the top of the food chain like sharks—the role given them by Nature. And here is the lesson of Nature to be remembered: *the day sharks die, a human catastrophe begins.*

Ultimate Equality

Did you get the visuals? This is the future that may be in store for all of us, rich or poor, when we get out of this bullet train called Equality and are still ... alive. But don't be in a hurry; the track does not end there. You see, one serious problem still remains: if the rich are pinched hard, they may leave the US and go somewhere else. Don't worry! There is a way how to prevent that from happening: go global to the ultimate destination.

The final stop of the bullet train is the station called *Ultimate Equality*. Now, you recognize the same voices: "Oh, how many poor people in Africa and the world." And here comes a bold and inspiring "we-are-the-world" proposal to equalize the income around the globe so that all people would live "in dignity."

The official goal is to help the poor nations, of course. But the real, hidden goal is to *redistribute wealth and thus ruin capitalism*. You see, the poverty-stricken, unappealing socialism living next door to the prosperous, attractive capitalism has no chances to attract anyone. Capitalism must be destroyed, preferably from inside; gradually, step by step. The progressives and socialists invented many ingenious schemes to do just that.

One of the schemes is foreign aid—a payoff to the poor Third World enforced by the "we-are-the-world" crowd in order to drain the resources of the rich capitalist nations. Although trillions have been spent to help the poor countries to stand on their feet, very little improvement has been achieved so far. Why do they need a fishing rod when the redistribution of tasty, cooked fish is going on, anyway?

Another scheme is to prolong the dependence of the capitalist countries on foreign oil. Oil trade has been the biggest transfer of wealth in the history of mankind from industrial capitalist economies into the Third World. It is steadily ruining capitalism and, thus, should be supported. Just let the militant environmentalists block any attempts to use coal; to find and produce domestic oil; or delay those attempts by diverting resources into renewable sources of energy. The renewable sources are not likely to reduce energy hunger for at least another 20 years or ever, but capitalism will be bludgeoned hard and bled significantly.

However, the Global Worming is the most arrogant and promising scheme designed to transfer wealth to the Third World and cripple capitalism. A new weapon against capitalism was found by the same environmentalists—an invisible gas carbon dioxide (CO_2). The authors of the scheme say: "The planet is endangered by global worming caused by excessive amounts of CO_2 released into the atmosphere by polluters; thus polluters should pay off the victims for their suffering."

And here, the Kioto Protocol appears sponsored by the United Nations. Who are those polluters? The wealthy capitalist countries, of course! They produce CO_2 and destroy the planet. (Well, they also produce goods and services as by-products that feed, dress, educate and entertain the planet, but it doesn't matter). Who are the victims? Mostly, they are the developing countries of the Third World that do not produce much, especially CO_2.

And here is the trick called "Clean Development Mechanism" (CDM) concocted to "motivate" the polluters to reduce (actually, to continue releasing) CO_2: the polluters should purchase from the victims, which never heard about CO_2, so-called carbon credits (a ransom as invisible as CO_2). In other words, pay the ransom and save the planet.

The poor Somali's fishermen (pirates) do the same: they offer the wealthy merchants to purchase their seized ships back. The same thing, except the Global Worming scheme covers the entire globe, not only the Indian Ocean. But at least, the pirates are honest. They say: "We are robbing you, not making the navigation safer."

The fraud of the Global Worming is evident everywhere: a caprice of Nature is claimed to be a man-made disaster; starving and drowning polar bears are starring in movies; climate data are manipulated to look like continuous warming. Oh, it is not worming! Sorry, honest mistake. Let's call it climate change. Then, it does not matter—worming, cooling or no change. Pay anyway; bleed capitalism to death and save the planet.

And when capitalism dies, the global income will be equalized at last. So, how much would everyone get (considering 2005 income)?

Just **$7,000**! That is how much every one of 6.7 billion people would receive out of the total world income of $46.9 trillion[4]. This is even less than the poor receive in the US! How can it be done? Just expropriate the income of the most productive and creative 19% of the Earth population[4] (about 1.3 billion) and spread it equally among the rest of the world.

Only then, the ultimate goal of Equality would finally be achieved: the rich will have no place to go and the class struggle will finally end. Well, everyone on the planet Earth will live...*below the poverty level!*

Just compare these numbers (see 2005 CBO table above):
Population:
World: 6.7 billion
US: 301 million (4.4% of the world population)
Total income:
World: $46.9 trillion
US: $9.7 trillion (20.6% of the world income)
Average income:
World: $7,000 per person (22% of US average income)
US: $32,000 per person.

"Look at this inequality!" The "we-are-the-world" crowd screams. "At the population of only 4%, the capitalist America has pocketed the outrageous 20% of the world income."

The implication is that Americans did not earn their income by respecting private property rights; embracing the free-market capitalism system; obeying the Constitution and cherishing freedoms; pursuing education; being talented and making discoveries; making innumerous inventions and implementing them; investing and taking risks; and by working harder than everyone else.

The implication is that their income does not belong to them; it was directly deposited in the imaginable *Global Equality Bank*. Then, the income was somehow fraudulently distributed, the poor nations being robbed from their fair share by the US and other capitalist countries.

Let me scream the truth at the top of my lungs: "The so hated free-market capitalist United States of America, the land of Ultimate Inequality, has created such unimaginable, unprecedented opportunity for its people!" Even the poor who do not work and live in poverty in the US are more prosperous than an average person living in 141 out of 213 countries of the world[5]." At global average income of $7,000, the poor in the US will become even poorer. They would be much better off living in the Land of Inequality.

But to accept inequality in the eyes of a socialist is much greater sin than to sentence everyone to poverty!

"That some should be rich shows that others may become rich, and hence is the encouragement to industry and enterprise. Let not him who is houseless pull down the house of another; but let him labor diligently and build one for himself."
Abraham Lincoln[6]

Chapter 3
NATURE VS. ALTRUISM

TERRA INCOGNITO "ALTRUISM

Big Hearts

It was the end of a hot summer of 1941, the first months of the horrible war. I was 4-year old at that time. My father was at the front as an officer in the Red Army, and my mom did not hear from him since the start of the war. She was trying desperately to find out where he was or if he was still alive. Most of the people packed their belongings and left the city of Kiev (Ukraine) where we lived because Germans came close and bombed the city every day. But mom did not want to leave. She was hopelessly waiting for my father to return and was afraid that he would not find us there.

One day, we were walking home on almost deserted streets when a miraculous chain of events happened that saved our lives. A military jeep came to a screeching stop next to us and a young officer called my mom by name. He served with my father before the war and recognized her.

"What are you doing here? Germans are surrounding the city!" He grabbed us into the jeep and drove us away to a freight train station on the outskirts of the city several hours before it was too late. There, we were standing on the platform among hundreds of panic-stricken people storming the last freight train. The officer brandishing a gun shoved us in a cattle car and the train took off heading to nowhere.

Several weeks later, we were dumped far away from home in an unfamiliar town—no warm clothes and no money; starving and homeless. But a local woman picked us up from the streets and brought us home. Her name was Maria, and she worked at a local hospital as a nurse. She gave us something to eat and allowed us to stay with her in her small room of a 2-story shabby apartment building. She also helped mom to find work at the hospital. Soon mom was washing soldier's dirty clothes and bloody linens 12 hours a day just for having one meal a day for both of us. When I got gravely ill and cried day and night, Maria's angry neighbors told her to kick us out back into the street. But the woman refused to do that. She told them that it was...*God's Will.* She virtually saved my life. Mom remembered this remarkable woman and her big heart all her life. But this is not the whole story.

At the end of the war, my family returned to Kiev. We lived in a small room of a 3-room apartment. Two other families occupied the other two rooms. One of our neighbors was an old widow. She was a fat and ugly woman known for her hateful character. She hated me and most of the kids from our building because we were making a lot of noise and mischief. She cursed us loudly wishing us tuberculosis, all kind of cancers and other deadly diseases. My mom had numerous altercations and did not speak with that woman because mom was superstitious. Boy, we hated that woman with all our guts.

She was not healthy and suddenly became seriously ill. At a hospital, she was diagnosed with an inoperable pancreatic cancer and brought back home to die. She was weak and lonely; her distant relatives lived far away and did not give a damn about her.

Then, something unexplainable happened. When the old woman returned from the hospital mortally ill, I could not recognize my Mom. She started cooking for that woman and hand-feeding her. She cleaned after her and even washed her soiled linen until the old woman died in a couple of months.

As a 12-year boy, I could not understand why mom did all this dirty work, while she worked so hard and cared for her own family at the same time. When I asked her, she replied that it was...*God's Will*.

I did not believe that: my mother was not religious. This story puzzled me at that time and later. During my wartime childhood, among misery and starvation, I saw many examples of indifference, selfishness, greed and cruelty. Therefore, the image of the compassionate nurse Maria was sparkling in my memory like a precious gem stone in a pile of dirt.

My mother had a big heart too. But did she help that old, sick woman because she was born that way or because she learned an unforgettable lesson from that nurse Maria who did not allow me to die in 1941?

To answer these seemingly simple questions turned out to be a difficult, life-long journey in search of an unknown land— terra incognito "Altruism."

Debate on the Plane

Almost life time has passed since those days. One day, I was flying from Chicago to San Diego on a business trip. I was sitting near the window next to two middle-aged passengers who seemed to know each other well. They were involved in an animated, intelligent conversation started obviously before they boarded the plane. They were discussing genetics and evolutionary biology, this kind of dull academic stuff. I was working on my presentation and did not pay much attention to what they were talking about until the younger fellow said:

"John, why don't you accept that animal altruism exists in nature? It is well documented in the literature based on studies of animal behaviors that some animals help each other. They also groom, warn and defend each other, you know. In fact, there are more altruists among animals than among people."

The word "animals" drew my attention instantly, and I pricked my ears. I love animals and stories about them.

"Milton, I do object," replied John cleaning his golden-rimmed glasses. "This so-called biological altruism has always been open to debates. It does not have sufficient explanatory power; it is not based on indisputable evidence and it has nothing to do with altruism per se."

"Is the evidence Hamilton brought in his "kin-selection" theory[1] not sufficient? Many animals behave altruistically (share food, for example) with their relatives, offspring, parents, siblings or cousins. They are involved in this altruistic self-sacrifice even if it reduces their fitness (chances to reproduce) in favor of those whom they help."

"Here is my problem, Milton. Helping kin relatives that share the same genetic codes is a selfish strategy. All of them are genetically similar and driven to propagate their genes at the expense of genes of others. What is altruistic about such behavior? These animals behave out of their genetic self-interest."

"I bet, you will reject also undisputable evidence presented by Trivers in his theory[2] of reciprocal altruism. The theory suggests that the animals receiving altruistic favors return the favor at some time. Such behavior evolves eventually in an inborn altruistic trait."

"What indisputable evidence do you have in mind?"

"A cleaner-fish is a good example. It gets inside the mouth of a much larger fish and cleans it from harmful parasites. Both fish make some sacrifice: the host does not swallow the cleaner-fish depriving itself a dinner, while the cleaner-fish does voluntary cleaning by eating those parasites."

"Milton, for God's sake, you are turning a fish into Mother Theresa! The large fish gets cleaned, and the smaller one gets fed. Is this altruistic behavior? Both fish behave in their self-interest—they expect a reward. Where is the altruism here? The whole deal is like you scratch my back and I scratch yours."

"Fine, what about birds that warn each other about the approaching predators. In fact, the whistle-blower exposes and put itself in danger to protect the group. Isn't this a real altruistic behavior?"

"Of course, it is not! Just the opposite! The whistle-blower is warning a predator that it was detected making itself safer in the first place. Recently, I was watching a scene from the Big Cat Diary on Animal Planet. They showed a leopard hiding behind the rocks watching a group of Thomson's gazelles. When he was ready to jump, one of the gazelles detected the predator and whistled. What do you think the leopard did? Jumped on the whistle-blower? No, it relaxed; muttered something like "my compliment to the chef" and walked away peacefully with his tail up.

You are an idealist, Milton. The animal altruism of yours is wishful thinking! Those behaviors can be explained by a concept of cooperation and self-interest as Nature intended. Now, let me ask you a question? *Why are you, guys, trying to shove altruism into any animal behavior so desperately?"*

"Would you like some beverage, Sir?" A flight attendant approached the combatants and interrupted this fascinating debate. I wish the pair to continue, but they switched to other topics, arguing with much less passion. Eventually, they aimed their noses at the screens of their laptops and later started reading some papers.

I was so mesmerized by the debate that I could not work anymore. I felt that it was not about animals; it was about something big I could not fully understand. This exchange was calm and civilized, but I felt some hidden intensity, a sign of something disturbing and menacing underneath. It was like crusted lava slowly flowing from a crater, a sign of the incredible inferno raging underground. It was like a small skirmish in a global clandestine war between two uncompromising camps.

John's last unanswered question was ringing in my ears: "Why are you, guys, trying to shove altruism into any animal behavior so desperately?" I decided to find the answer to this question myself.

Different Faces of Altruism

I always believed that the idea of altruism was synonymous to the idea of helping people, just sounds more intelligent and scientific. What is so complicated about helping people, anyway? Help is when you see it. Boy, I was so wrong! There are obviously other sides of altruism I did not know, and the concept of helping people turned out to be not as simple as I always thought. In fact, it has always been viewed differently by different people.

For example, St. Thomas Aquinas[3], a 13th century philosopher, believed that in helping people *we should love ourselves more than our neighbors.* I could not agree more. My mother was known to help people often. But she would have never taken a piece of bread out of my mouth to give it away.

However, to love yourself more than your neighbor has not always been sufficient for some people. When it comes to helping others, the Bible[4] demands much more sacrifice from the believers. It teaches that *"you should love your neighbor as yourself."*

But for those who feel that this is still not enough, a 19th century French philosopher Auguste Comte carried the concept of helping others to extremes. He was the first to introduce the term "altruism" to describe his altruistic doctrine. Here is how Comte[5] described it:

"While it is important to acknowledge the innateness (presence from birth) of the sympathetic (altruistic) instincts, one is forced to admit their native weakness: the supremacy of the egoistic tendencies is so clear that it is itself one of the most striking traits in our nature. The great human problem is to reverse the natural order and to teach ourselves to live for others."

In other words, Comte altruism consists of two main concepts:

The 1st concept recognizes that altruism and egoism are both inborn human traits. Altruism is desirable, but a very weak trait, while undesirable egoism is so strong that it suppresses the altruism.

The 2nd concept states that Nature is wrong; Man can and should change Nature through teaching and learning altruism, which is a duty and moral obligation to live for the sake of others even at a sacrifice of your own self-interest.

Thus, *"live-for-others" altruism* has always been the original, authentic meaning of the term altruism.

"Live-for-others" altruism (LFO altruism, for short) attracted and influenced many philosophers of its time, including Karl Marx. The main attraction has always been in its potential appeal to self-sacrifice and to change human nature. Remember Marx's famous saying: "The philosophers have only interpreted the world in various ways: the point, however, is to change it."

The dominance of LFO altruism was established from the "top down" in the 20th century. It was enforced as an official ethical doctrine in totalitarian, collectivist, fascist, socialist and communist ideologies and eventually states. It became a powerful tool to force people to live and sacrifice themselves for the sake of others—an ideology, a party or a government. As a dominant social doctrine, Comte altruism was glorified and violently propagated down into every fabric of social life, especially science, philosophy and academia.

After the world-wide collapse of totalitarian, collectivist, fascist, socialist and communist ideologies, millions of people who escaped the killing fields told the world the truth about the LFO altruistic societies and the influence of the concept plunged to a catastrophic level.

It became very difficult to advertise openly and sell LFO altruism. It is in disguise now hiding under noble names "*moralistic*" altruism or "*ethical*" altruism. But how moral or ethical this doctrine has been in practice?

All Rise! The Nature's Court is in Session! LFO Altruism vs. Reality!

In the eyes of Nature, the LFO altruism is an absurdity, but it is not evident to most people until it is too late—until every one is forced to live for others (that is for the Government) like in the former USSR.

Therefore, let's resort to an allegory to clearly illustrate this point. Let's imagine that the proponents of the LFO altruism are complaining about the morals of the capitalist society. They present a seemingly valid and convincing case in favor of the LFO altruism in the Circuit Court of…Nature.

"All rise! Nature's Court is in session! Honorable Judge Nature is presiding. LFO Altruism vs. Reality!"

"Your Honor, we are genuinely concerned about the morals of the capitalist society based on egoism and self-interest. People care only about themselves; they are prisoners of acquisitiveness and greed and thus, devoid of genuine freedom.

We want to build an altruistic society, in which people live for others and care about others more than about themselves."

"But many people have been helping others voluntarily in egoistic societies for centuries, and they will continue to do so if they wish," Judge Nature remarks.

"Your Honor, we want a society, in which everyone has no choice, but to help others. Society cannot depend on voluntarism; people must be connected to each other and coerced to do right things in order to achieve genuine freedom and happiness."

"Will everyone be free, happy and connected in that society?" the Judge asks.

"Absolutely, Your Honor. Everyone will be if the existing egoistic society is destroyed. We have a theory of socio-economic justice which predicts just that."

"But if the altruistic society is so good and appealing, why are people not fleeing the egoistic society?"

"Your Honor, people are ignorant, stupid and lazy by nature; they need progressive intellectuals to lead them to water. We know better what people need."

"If people are ignorant and lazy by nature, they may be acquisitive, egoistic and greedy by nature too. How are you going to convince all of them to follow you voluntarily if human nature is against it?

"Our theory provides effective, practical methods of convincing people to follow, Your Honor. We will link people together and convince them to sign a voluntary altruistic contract."

"But the opponents contend that such altruistic society cannot exist unless people are brutally forced to live in it," the Judge objects.

"Those are the excuses to justify living under such horrible morality, your Honor."

"Did you consider all the consequences?" Judge warns.

"Yes, your Honor, we did. Our theory predicts genuine freedom and happiness for everyone."

"Fine, do it at your peril, but I take a disclaimer," Judge Nature says. Nature has never been against those taking risk as long as it goes with taking responsibility.

And the proponents of the LFO altruism did it against Nature's warning and corralled people in one place. They linked them to each other...with chains, thus convincing them to sign a basic, altruistic, socialist contract. In the contract, *"Government promises to make the world a better place to live and you agree to live for the sake of others."*

The terms and conditions of the contract (written in small print) were also appealing. The contract reads:

"You surrender to others your home and possessions; your labor and talents; your thoughts, choices and wishes; your body and even your life. They do not belong to you any longer; they belong to others (the Government).

You surrender to others all your decisions too: where to live and how much space you need; what you can buy and what you can sell; what profession you can choose and where you can work; how much money you can make and how much you can keep; what clothes you can wear and how you wear it; what you can say and what you can hear; what books you can read and what your children should be taught; whom you should love and whom you should hate; and on, and on, and on; and finally how, when and where you have to die to force others to live for others."

This is a snap-shot of a real altruistic society based on "live-for-others" altruism. Wait a minute! How, in the world, did all those people agree to sign such contract? How could they live under such nightmarish conditions? Simple: *they are the only ones who are not dead.* For curious: you cannot get out of this non-revocable contract ever. *It is for the rest of your life!* The "better place to live" was surrounded by barbed wires and guarded by other armed LFO altruists like you.

In fact, the Government does not really care whether you are a genuine LFO altruist. You can be a hidden egoist as long as you behave as a "live/die-for-Government" altruist. As a result, the altruistic society is a perfect breeding ground for skillful pretenders and hidden egoists who act accordingly when no one is watching. Just look at the communist leaders who call every one to sacrifice and live for others; but they never miss an opportunity to backstab each other (like spiders in a jar) to advance their status and position selfishly.

This is what academia calls the altruistic society, the world that is a better place to live (for others). They come to these conclusions by experimenting with laboratory mice at Ivy League universities.

Unfortunately, the truth revealed by the prisoners released from the LFO altruistic concentration camps did not make this discredited philosophy disappear. It has been entrenched in academia and is progressively creeping back. This time, the opposite, "bottom-up" strategy is used to revive the LFO altruism—from corridors of academia up to corridors of power. The new tactics is to spread (intentionally or not) three main myths about altruism. Here are my thoughts about that.

MYTH 1: ALTRUISM IS HELPING OTHERS

What is "Real" Altruism?

A famous American writer and philosopher Ayn Rand exposed the vicious nature of live-for-other altruism half a century ago. It was the time when it was at the height of its popularity among left-wing intellectuals. At that time, altruism meant what it was supposed to mean—LFO altruism as was intended by its author Auguste Comte and everyone else sympathetic to socialist ideals. Ayn Rand clearly understood that LFO altruism had nothing to do with kindness or generosity; that it was an irreplaceable tool in the hands of progressives in their seemingly unstoppable march toward socialism. However, no one could anticipate a complete break-up of the socialist economic and political systems at that time. So, what is happening to LFO altruism today? Here is an update.

Now, when the philosophy of LFO altruism was discredited and fell from grace, the proponents of altruism are trying to distance themselves from it (temporarily). They switched to another form of altruism called *"real"* altruism. They say that *live-for-others* altruism is too extreme, and it may give altruism a bad name now. Real altruism is kindness, benevolence, compassion and generosity—all these noble acts of helping people in one.

That's what bothers me. The genuine meaning of altruism is to live for *others,* which has nothing to do with the noble acts of helping *other.* These facts are widely recognized by *others,* even by the former proponents of LFO altruism. Then, why are these proponents still desperately clinging to the term altruism? Oh, it originates from Italian word *altrui,* which means...*others.*

So, what is "real" altruism, anyway? Let's start with animals first. Yes, that's right; there is a definition of altruism specifically crafted for animals. For example, Wikipedia (Altruism in animals) reads: altruism is *"an act, in which an animal sacrifices its own well-being for the benefits of another animal."*

Now, compare it with a widely accepted definition of altruism in humans. It is described as *"unselfish or selfless regard or devotion to* (per Encyclopedia Britannica, Merriam-Webster Dictionary) or *concern for* (per Wikipedia, Altruism) *the welfare of others."*

Surprisingly, it does not call altruism an *action*; it does not call for a *sacrifice* either. It calls just for *regard, devotion or concern* that is for consideration or respect; dedication or commitment; worry or interest, but not for direct actions and sacrifices.

Is this fair? To become altruists, animals have to sacrifice, while people need to have just good intentions. Why do they give humans a slack, while demanding more from animals? I find these requirements discriminative, abusive and cruel to poor animals as well as quite suspicious.

Why does not the definition of real altruism call for actions and sacrifices? May be, it is done for political reasons: actions and sacrifice are the mandatory requirements for discredited LFO altruism, and they may smear the image of real altruism by association.

Regardless of reasons, without actions and sacrifices (giving up something valuable or important), altruism cannot help others. It cannot claim even to be a pledge; it becomes just a meaningless intention. Would you call me a real altruist if I tell you how devoted I am to and concerned about some charity without giving them a dime? You would call me a fake.

Just look at the real acts of big-heartedness or kindness; look at what the nurse Maria did saving my life or what my mother did helping a dying old woman. Both women acted, sacrificed and did not expect any rewards.

If real altruism is all those noble things, the definition of real altruism should also include these criteria: *actions, self-sacrifice and selfless motivation.* We expect from humans at least as much as from animals.

Now we are talking, you may say! Not so fast! Even if all these criteria are met, real altruism is still too confusing to understand and live by. This makes me think that "real altruism" is an artificial concept that intentionally concocted not to help others, but to confuse others in order to follow a hidden agenda (we will get back to this later).

Does Real Altruism Mean Helping Others?

Anyway, whether defined intentionally or not, real altruism is not a substitute for the concept of helping others. There are too many problems (not semantic, of course) that arise immediately when a family of noble human traits related to helping others is replaced with single generic term altruism. Here is why.

How much sacrifice do you have to make to become a real altruist? On one extreme, let's say, you possess much more than your neighbor (the case: rich vs. poor) and you share voluntarily a small portion of what you have with him. All criteria of altruism are met—actions, voluntarism and sacrifice (small sacrifice is still sacrifice). So, is this real altruism? Yes, it is—by definition. O-o-ops! Now, the greedy rich may look like real altruists, even better altruists than most of us. No, we cannot call this case altruism; let's call it Charity. Now, we've got an exception—charity of the rich is not real altruism.

Let's say, you possess as much as your neighbor does and you both belong to a middle class as majority of us. Does it make you a real altruist if you share some of what you have voluntarily with your neighbor? Yes, it does—by definition. But your neighbor may be offended because it has a negative connotation if you are on the receiving end of altruism. He may prefer to consider it as an act of g*ood will or kindness*. He may well reject your help feeling obligated to reciprocate equally. And if he does reciprocate, he does not do it voluntarily, out of his free will. Now, you are both equally compensated; getting no help; and making no voluntary sacrifice. Still, it will be considered real altruism although it looks like mutual aid.

And on another extreme, you starve and give away the last piece of bread to your starving neighbor voluntarily. You die to let somebody live. This is also real altruism by definition. Really! You just traded your life for someone else's. Is the neighbor's life more valuable than yours? Do your starving kids need your neighbor's life more than yours?

Here, altruism contradicts Nature. Nature gets rid of such altruists to prevent them from breeding. Only selfish cheaters, who do not reciprocate, survive. It is confusing, isn't it? But there is another problem.

Is your motivation selfless enough? Selflessness is the second criterion of real altruism, and it is even more confusing. The giver's motivation is often difficult to verify—people typically have many reasons to hide their motives.

Does your altruistic act make you feel good from receiving gratitude and praises? If so, this mean that you do it for your own pleasure or satisfaction; that you expect this pleasure in exchange. This is real egoism, not selflessness. Lie about your real motive and bask in the sunlight of real altruistic honor.

Do you expect your neighbor to reciprocate? If so, this is a business deal made in your own self-interest rather than selflessness.

Are you trying to win friends or a favorable opinion of yourself? This is not altruism, as well. This is bribery or vanity.

And finally, are you involved because of peer pressure; because you are obligated or forced to do it by others (a group of people or a government)? This is not real altruism if it is not voluntary; if you try to avoid social shame or a peer pressure; or if you do it out of fear for your life.

Unfortunately, those are examples of real altruism although they defy common sense and sometimes are shameful.

Wait a minute! I would add *the fourth criterion* missing in the modern definition of real altruism by some reasons. The voluntary help and sacrifice of a giver *should be welcomed by and should not be harmful to a recipient*. Help should not be shoved into your throat against your will by others!

Ayn Rand put it categorically[6]: "Only individual men have the right to decide when and whether they wish to help others; society—as an organized political system—has no rights in the matter at all."

And here is the main point: helping others is a noble act, which has always been and will always be practiced by Man voluntarily; it must never be turned into coerced altruism by others for the sake of others!

In conclusion, the modern definition of real altruism, intentionally or not, is concocted to be too general, vague, incomplete, confusing and misleading. It allows hardly altruistic acts to be claimed as altruistic. In this respect, the popularization and over usage of the term altruism in scientific and non-scientific literature and everyday language is rather intentional and suspicious.

The term altruism is not a legitimate term to describe human behavior aimed at helping others. There are many other legitimate terms to describe that. The term "help," "aid" or "assistance" is equally good for that purpose. For example, how does it sound: a theory of evolutionary help; a concept of kin aid; or a hypothesis of reciprocal" assistance?

No matter how many new definitions are concocted for the term *altruism,* it will forever be branded, recognized and associated with the vicious *"live-for-others" altruism* as was intended originally 160 years ago by its author French philosopher Auguste Comte.

Real Altruism is the Trojan Horse!

There is a concerted effort to make the term "real altruism" the only legitimate term to describe the concept of helping others. (It is called just "altruism" nowadays, for the sake of simplicity, of course). If the idea of altruism is planted in your mind as the only one associated with idea of helping others, then it will help exonerate LFO altruism eventually. Let's see how this scheme works.

At first glance, to dump all the meanings of helping others into one term altruism looks rather innocent and not deceptive. For millenniums, the concept of helping others has been known and dear to Man's heart through religious or personal experience. This multi-sided concept describes numerous ways and forms of helping people. It is based on a family of noble, learned human traits such as bigheartedness, benevolence, kindness, selflessness, compassion, generosity, charitableness and others.

It is hard to suspect that the scheme calling all of them just altruism is an intricate fallacy. Intentional or not, this fallacy is spread around by academia and sympathetic or ignorant media to pursue a sinister agenda to make LFO altruism look respectable again.

Allegorically speaking, this fallacy is a psychological drama "Wolf in Sheep's Clothing." The sheep's clothing is the concept of helping others; the wolf is the term real altruism. So, what is the scenario of this drama?

In the 1st act, the audience gets used to the notion that HELPING OTHERS = REAL ALTRUISM. All individual actions of humans or animals aimed at helping others are claimed to be and called altruism. Any related concept, motivation or behavior, is broadly described as altruistic, from the bird's warning calls to justification of the welfare state. All positive images of helping people are now associated with the notion of altruism. Altruism is becoming a synonym of the concept of helping others. Eventually, real altruism hijacks and usurps the very meaning of this noble concept.

In the 2nd act, the perception that REAL ALTRUISM = LFO ALTRUISM is introduced, methodically reiterated and reinforced until the audience believes that both of them are related like brothers. Well, both of them have the same last name "altruism," aren't they? So, let's call both of them just altruism. Not a big deal. But an invisible transformation is taking place, which makes people feel good about LFO altruism. It is like you ask a person you just met:

"Did you say your name was Johnson? Are you related, by any chance, to my dear friend Sam Johnson who helped me during difficult times?"

"Yes, I am his brother." And warm sympathy toward that unknown person and the desire to embrace him fill your heart right away.

And here is the most anticipated Finale—the audience is made to believe that LFO ALTRUISM = HELPING OTHERS by association with real altruism. Now, LFO altruism is embraced as the only form of helping others; it does not matter how—by expropriating the rich, high taxes or confiscating private property by the government.

Today, we are watching the third act of this play—most of us see no difference between LFO altruistic actions and voluntary, noble acts of helping others. We call it just altruism. We are encouraged to live for others. Now, this is not academic issue any more; it is the sobering reality.

You still don't believe that our country is moving toward socialism. Let's check if some legislative acts lead us there. Let's trace them to their roots—a socialist ideal of altruism, which will be achieved when most of us live for others.

When the Government "spreads the wealth around" without your consent through higher taxes to help others (less fortunate)—this is the LFO altruism in action. And if you don't feel violated, let's make it visual: your neighbor takes your money from the bank without your permission and gives it to a charity of his choice. Oh, now you do feel violated!

When the Government pressures the banks to give and then forgive mortgages, tuition or credit card loans to others (the disadvantaged) who, they know, will never repay them—this is the LFO altruism in action. Oh, you still don't care! Let's make it visual: you earned this money and put it in the bank for safe keeping, but the bank without your permission gives it away to the disenfranchised). Oh, now you do care!

When the Government tries to help others (uninsured) through higher insurance premiums you pay and lower standard of medical care you get—this is the LFO altruism in action. Oh, now you are screaming! Good!

In other words, such psychological drama can help to replace a noble concept of helping others in your mind with a vicious concept of living for others. Real altruism, like the "Trojan horse, helps a small group of people manipulate the masses of people into living for others.

MYTH 2: ALTRUISM IS INBORN TRAIT

Is Altruism an Inborn Trait? Who cares?

Altruism has been one of the most discussed and studied concepts. You can find altruism in social science, philosophy; biology, psychology, anthropology, sociology, neurobiology, ethology, you name it. You can find altruism in every form and shape there: real altruism, reciprocal altruism, kin altruism, competitive altruism, empathy altruism, evolutionary altruism and many others. It is like a restaurant menu: baked potato, fried potato, mash of potato, roasted potato—potato for any taste.

For millenniums, people managed to help each other; they were benevolent, kind, selfless, compassionate, generous or charitable and did not call their noble àcts altruism. Only in the ideological 19th and 20th centuries, there was uncontrolled proliferation of the term altruism, to explain animal and human behaviors. This is not accidental and innocent as it may seem.

But who cares? This issue is so academic and so remote to everyday life, isn't it? Wrong! The proponents of altruism are waging an uncompromised war propagating another fallacy—to legitimize the 1st Comte concept and to prove that *altruism is an inborn trait*. They say that altruism is not just a theory born in a little human mind, which may err and fail; altruism is a natural phenomenon created, propagated and sponsored by Mother-Nature herself that never fails. They say that altruism exists and is wide spread in living nature, from highly intelligent animals to plants. All living creatures are capable of learning altruism; moreover, they are born as altruists passing their "altruistic" genes through heredity.

This explains an explosion of research studies on biological altruism being conducted so desperately. The researchers have been trying to find altruistic behaviors and altruistic genes in humans, animals, warms, plants, tree roots, you name it.

Why? Here is the agenda hidden from the naked eye. The goal is to prove that biological altruism exists, and it is more advantageous strategy for existence of living things in Nature than self-interest is. The obvious and inescapable conclusion for humans is that *the structure of a human society based on altruism is more advantageous than that based on self-interest or egoism.* Then, it is justified *to apply LFO altruism to a human society again*; to force everyone to be selfless and sacrifice oneself for the sake of a state, its ideology and ideologues. But for this to happen, the biological altruism has to be sold to the public as scientific "truth."

Most scientists study the laws of the natural world (hard science) and incredible inventions of Nature trying to duplicate them. Each theory is experiment-verifiable and reproducible before it is implemented. The discovered "truth" about the natural world is objective; there is no room for guessing or interpretation. If a theory right, it works, benefits Man, and it lives. If it is wrong, it is discarded before it does any harm.

But there is another branch of science (soft science). Among other things, it studies the relationships between people and develops theories that show the ways Man has to live. And here is a problem. Man is a living thing of incredible complexity and the relationships between people are even more complex as intended by Nature. Man does not have enough intellectual capacity to comprehend these complexities and the purpose of Nature. So, the scientists resort to approximations as a substitute for the objective "truth" about humanity. As a result, this "truth" is subjective and unreliable; it is based on incomplete and inconclusive information or open-ended assumptions; on personal opinions and interpretations.

Marx and Lenin did exactly that. They believed that wisdom of Man is superior to wisdom of Nature and tried to correct "errors" made by Nature. They claimed that they knew the one and the only "truth" about how Man had to live called socialism. This "truth" was not experiment-verifiable and reproducible before it was implemented. When it was implemented, it could not be abandoned even when it appeared to be false. And the harm inflicted on Man became known only after many decades of suffering, bloodshed and millions of lost lives.

But the world has changed, and the Marx's "truth" that defies Nature was discredited even in the eyes of his followers and sympathizers. Now, they have chosen a new tactic. They have eventually come to recognize the power of Nature's wisdom; they are trying to enlist Nature's support to prove their theories motivated by philosophical bias. The same scientists who believe in and are searching tirelessly for the "altruistic" genes will strongly deny the existence of the "egoistic" genes; never look for them or ignore them if they were found.

Nowadays, there is real "golden rush" in search of altruistic genes in animals. And if you look for something hard enough, you will find it even if it is not there; even in humans. And what a surprise! Recently, Israeli scientists have reportedly found an "altruistic" gene in humans. German scientists followed suit declaring also that they found an "altruistic" gene, and a link between altruism and heredity.

How was Altruistic Gene Found?

The "altruistic" gene in humans was discovered by the German scientists headed by Dr. Martin Reuter at the University of Bonn. It was widely reported and celebrated in the media as a breakthrough in science. I looked up their article published on line in October 2010 on PhysOrg[7] to see how the altruistic gene was found. Let me briefly describe this study to show how the proponents of altruism are trying to sell it to the public.

A small group of "Caucasian students of German origin" (101 students, for curious) from the same university was given 5€ (about $7) each for participating in a fake memory test. After the test, they were also given (through fake gambling) a small sum in coins as an endowment for an optional charity donation. The anonymity of the participants was "pretended" also. The magnitude of donation was used as the measure of altruism. Then, the researchers made a genetic analysis of each student and a statistical analysis of the data to determine whether one of two variations of a gene called COMT is responsible for altruistic behavior in people. (Of course, COMT had nothing to do with Comte—the author of LFO altruism, but the coincidence was symbolic and full of irony).

The sensational conclusion was that the students-carriers of the gene COMT Val donated *twice as much* as the carriers of the gene COMT Met. The news was immediately spread by the media as a clear indication that COMT Val is the illusive altruistic gene. Thus, altruism was linked to heredity, which was the undeclared goal of the study. This article is a typical example how the myths about altruism are created by bias academia and ignorant media. Let me show you what they do not want you to know.

In the article, the authors do not even conceal their bias views. They accept the predominant liberal view that altruism is a "pro-social" behavior. It implies that a non-altruistic behavior (like self-interest) is antisocial. The authors believe that when people are "preoccupied with their problems" (care about their needs), such behavior is not acceptable.

Moreover, pro-social behavior is claimed to be a "prerequisite for the growth and prosperity of societies." It implies that a capitalist society based on self-interest cannot grow and be as prosperous as an altruistic, socialist society can be, for example. The students were told that the recipient of their donations is not a faceless charity, but a real person: a poor (undoubtedly starving) little girl (with a pretty name Lina) with a sympathetic (but sad) face (a real photo was provided) in a known poor country (Peru). Thus, the students were given a hint and intimidated psychologically. What a monster are you if you do not want to help this starving child?

It was claimed that the students felt that they donated "hard-earned" money. But the students are not that stupid to realize that it is free and easy money earned by playing games and gambling! Easy comes—easy goes. A couple of dollars given to the students was not hard to donate; it was such unnoticeable sacrifice for them; they spent more on booze or parties. How low the devaluation of altruism can go if you want to prove your point so desperately?

But here is the catch! Despite the unduly influence, the students-carriers of the "altruistic" gene ("real altruists") donated on average only 43% of the money, while non-carriers (egoists, I presume) donated only 22%—t*wice as less*! That is what academia wants you to see! But why didn't the pitiful "generosity" (43%) embarrass the authors? Instead, they dropped the bar so low that they could present COMT Val as a real (not faked) "altruistic" gene. Now, they can claim that the carriers of that gene are real (not faked) altruists, as well.

Here is more! The authors didn't advertise the fact that only pathetic 23% of all the students-carriers of the "altruistic" gene donated all their money; while some of them donated nothing! Why didn't at least majority of those fake altruists give away at least most of their money, which, in fact, was not even theirs? Why did they keep more for themselves than they donated?

Just think about how the facts can be twisted! The carriers of a weak altruistic gene COMT Val have pocketed 57% of the money, and the authors called them real, inborn altruists. Then, how would you call the carriers of a strong gene COMT Met who have pocketed a whopping 78%? Inborn egoists?

"Guys, are you sure you've found the altruistic gene? Oh, you are not sure! Then, congrats are in order—*you have found the egoistic gene by mistake*! Liberal academia has provided evidence that people are born predominantly as egoists! What an embarrassing situation for the authors and the sponsors! Thanks a lot! The question still remains though: did such competent researchers miss these facts inadvertently or they preferred to ignore them? What do you think?

The authors themselves did not feel much confidence in the results due to many shortcomings of their study. They admitted that this "study is explorative"; that the number of participants was much smaller than required; that the students were not checked for their social and economic backgrounds. Eventually, the authors confess that they "do not argue against the need for an independent replication study."

But this is not all. How about not checking the ideological views of the students participating in such ideologically-driven study conducted by the ideologically-driven researchers—the credibility of the data may be tainted! How about selecting more diverse group of students to avoid suspicions that the bias authors may be their teachers—the objectivity of the tested students may be in question! How about giving some credit to the students—they could figure out that the fake (sorry "pretended") anonymity may reveal their identity. Would you risk your reputation for a couple of bucks?

So, what we learned from this sensational, but extremely bias and flawed study? Did this "explorative" experiment find an altruistic gene and a clear connection between altruism and heredity?

Give me a break! A serious research conducted by qualified researchers found what was not there and ignored what was there. The authors gave their sponsor some advice about "the future direction in the altruism research." Here is my advice. How about looking for the egoistic genes for a change? Oh, it is too late to advise—you may have already found it. How about asking students to donate their own money instead of somebody else's to show their natural (not faked) generosity or altruism? Bad advice too—you may never find any altruistic genes then. How about conducting cleaner research neutral to a liberal political agenda? Ignorant advice again—you wouldn't probably get money for such research!

Thus, unnoticed by most people, a cold war has been raging on—a psychological, ideological battle to revive Comte "live-for-others" altruistic doctrine. I heard the echo of this battle on the plane flying from Chicago to the West coast when John asked Milton: "Why are you, guys, trying to shove altruism into any animal behavior so desperately?" I think I've found the answer to that question now. Wait a minute! I have found a convincing illustration too!

About Blackie, the Cat and the Lazy Bums

I have always been a hard-core cat lover. When I was a young man in my previous life, I used to bring stray cats home. But after one of them died from rabies, I along with my parents received 20-30 painful shots each in the stomach. So, I promised my parents that I would never do it again. Still one of the cats, lived with us for 13 years. One day, she brought a litter of four adorable kittens. We found people who adapted two of them soon, but two other kittens stayed with us for five months more.

They lived in the kitchen and slept in a basket with their mom. They ate from the same saucer I filled with food every day. The kittens were well fed and pampered; they were fatty, fluffy and slept a lot. The lazy bums played together, shared food and never quarreled over it. They were really "altruistic" cats, by nature.

One fall evening, I was walking home after visiting my grandma. It was cold and wet. The only thing on my mind was how to get home fast and get warm. Suddenly, I saw an abandoned kitten about 4-month old shivering on the pavement. No one in the street paid attention to the desperate kitty. I stopped and looked at him. He was black and dirty; thin and wet; hopeless eyes and drooping little ears.

"I cannot take you home, little Blackie? I have already two like you. And then, rabies, my mother and my promise, you know." I patted him on the head and walked away thinking about my clumsy excuse, luck and justice in this world. When I stopped at an intersection, I heard meowing. Here, he was sitting next to me, a small ball of fading life. The cat wanted to live; he did not accept my excuses and followed me to the very door of my apartment. He broke my heart, and I snuck him into a warm kitchen. Here, he was introduced to my two little lazy bums and their mom, all three watching him with disgust and suspicion.

What happened next came as a shocking manifestation of Nature's wisdom and started a serious philosophical discussion in my mind. The hungry Blackie rushed to the food. He started clearing the saucer with an amazing speed as the astonished cats were watching and hissing in desperation. Well, the lazy bums went to sleep without supper this night. But the real shock came the next day when I filled saucer with new food. Yesterday, my little, lazy bums were altruists and shared food. Now, they jumped to the saucer without invitation. They blocked and pushed each other growling and trying to get as much food as they can at the expense of each other.

The world of the two "civilized" kittens and their "manners" had changed forever since that day. I thought they were born kind and generous by their nature. Not at all! The kittens learned that there was always plenty of food, so they shared it and became close pals. But it took only several dramatic minutes to shutter the feline rosy world and erase their "altruistic" learned behavior. One lesson on competition from Mother-Nature and their hidden so far egoism kicked in.

Does it look familiar? People drop their altruistic masks also in extreme situations (food shortage, famine, shipwreck, wars, etc.). Which brings us back to the same question: are animals, including Man, altruists or egoists by nature?

Altruism or Egoism?

So, it looks like the "altruistic" behavior of those kittens is a temporary, learned behavior; while egoism is permanent and inherited. In other words, "you can take a wolf out of the forest, but you cannot take forest out of the wolf."

Even Comte in his "live-for-others" altruistic doctrine recognized that people are born with *three weak altruistic traits, and seven strong egoistic traits.* In other words, people are born predominantly as egoists! Remember the two genes Dr. Reuter found—one sickly altruistic and one strongly egoistic? Altruism is like a thin film covering a solid egoistic base. Why is that?

In contrast to grooming, warning calls and babysitting (arbitrarily considered altruistic behaviors in animals), sharing food is a real and incontestable manifestation of altruism because it is life-threatening during food shortage or famine: you share; you starve; you die and do not pass your genes to the next generation. Not sharing food is an egoistic act; but it is not life-threatening. Therefore, egoism, not altruism, must have been a prevailing, dominant behavior in animals and primordial homos/humans for millions of years.

Like a shower of sediments (organic and non-organic matter suspended in water) that sinks to the ocean floor and petrifies (turns into stone) with time, these egoistic everyday events were accumulated and became a solid inborn trait *Egoism* passed from generation to generation.

An animal may altruistically share food only when food is abundant; when such altruism does not result in hunger; and when the survival of an individual is not threatened. I remember a scene from the popular TV series about the Planet Earth. Here, a male polar bear, after having gorged himself at the kill, reluctantly allowed a stranger female starving for weeks to have the leftovers. The reason of this rare act is not known, but some people may call it altruistic. Then, why did the male repeatedly threaten and chase off the female when he was still hungry?

Theoretically, altruism may become an inborn trait if such altruistic events are accumulated uninterrupted for a long time. But this is extremely unlikely. Periods of food abundance and famine take turns in Nature. Periods of food abundance are rare due to lack of resources on such small planet like Earth. They do not last long either due to the resulting overpopulation. Thus, food shortage is a predominant phenomenon in Nature—a wise Nature's balancing strategy to prevent species from gorging themselves out of existence.

A satiated animal can afford to share food altruistically for a relatively long time if there is plenty of food around. In contrast, during food shortage, sharing is dangerous—only days of hunger and those who share (altruists) are gone. Those who do not share (egoists) survive. At the first signs of food shortage, altruism (accumulated during the previous period of food abundance) is immediately erased, and the naked base of egoism (developed over much longer periods of food shortages) is exposed. Egoism is always on standby underneath of altruism; at the first signs of hunger, egoism is called to the rescue.

So, in Nature, contrary to egoism, altruism in sharing resources can be observed in animals (and typically in humans) only temporarily when resources are in abundance and the survival of animals (and humans) is not endangered.

Are Animals Real Altruists Like People?

Behavior of animals has nothing to do with altruism—it is just self-interest. That is what John showed during the debate I overheard on the plane. He raised reasonable doubts that biological altruism in animals exists, while Milton failed to prove otherwise.

There are numerous reported cases about so-called altruistic animals such as fish cleaning other fish[8]; vampire bats sharing food[9]; monkeys giving warning calls[10]; and many others. There are also numerous cases of altruism in animals I read about on the Internet or watched on TV (wolves regurgitating meat for the members of their pack and cubs; dolphins helping the injured dolphins; monkeys grooming each other; etc.).

However, all these claims of altruism, in fact, could well be explained as self-interest of the living creatures; as an intention to help themselves and their off-springs by strengthening the pack in a deadly struggle for their own survival and propagation. I love those altruistic claims, especially grooming: you scratch my back and I will scratch yours. Scratching somebody's hairy back is how low the bar was set for an altruistic behavior.

But here is the most ridiculous case[11] I found lately on the Internet. It is about "altruistic"…amoebae from a cellular *slime* mould family called Dictyostelium mucoroides (what a noble name for a disgusting slime!). They can live only in *dead* plants. When *starved*, these amoebae join up into a tiny *slug,* and some of them (just listen to this academic interpretation) *sacrifice themselves for the sake of other amoebae.* This sensational conclusion comes from the fact that some amoeba die, and the spores of other amoebae use their dried bodies to transport themselves through the air.

Do the brainless amoebae voluntarily sacrifice themselves? Let me offer more realistic explanation. When food runs out, some of the "kamikazes" probably starve to death; some are killed in a mortal combat for survival or cannibalized by others, the strongest among them.

Sacrifice themselves for others! Does it sound familiar? Is this a local amoebae branch of "live-for-others" altruistic society? I imagine the appeal for ignorant people: "Even amoebae have embraced LFO altruism!"

Just think what academia tries to portray as altruism: *a slimy, sluggish (and therefore starving) society, in which everything around is dead or rotten, and the members are cannibalized by others for the sake of others!* Thanks academia, for giving us a descriptive definition of a socialist society based on LFO altruism.

Why bring altruism at all when one of the criteria of real altruism (selfless, conscious motivation) cannot be applied to animals, plants or amoebae; when those behaviors could be explained by a concept of cooperation dictated by their own self-interest in a struggle for survival as Nature intended? It is obvious that the distortion of the definition and devaluation of the meaning of real altruism is needed to fit a hidden agenda.

Those who selected altruism as an example to prove that human behavior evolves through evolutionary mechanism have selected a wrong example. Real altruism cannot evolve in Nature; it contradicts the laws of Nature unless altruism is devalued to scratching somebody's back. But grooming is not on animals' mind during the famine—the survival is. Famine is a real test of altruism. Even Darwin realized this undeniable fact.

Those who are trying to prove at any cost that behaviors of animals and amoebae are altruistic and inherent do this because the stakes are high: they are trying to lure ordinary people to become altruists. And this is just a matter of time before these new altruists (and all others) are corralled into the LFO altruistic hard-labor camps surrounded with barbed wires and observation towers.

MYTH 3: ALTRUISTIC SOCIETY IS THE FUTURE

Is Altruistic Society a Fantasy?

Great thinkers, from ancient philosophers to modern social scientists, were trying to find the way how to rid people of egoism and self-interest, entirely and for good. In fact, there is no problem to build a prosperous society based on self-interest. People do not have to learn how to care about their own needs; they are born this way. I risked my life for the privilege to live with my family in one of those societies. Millions of others did the same.

But altruism is different; you should learn how to care about others. If altruism is an inborn, but weak trait suppressed by egoism as Comte believed, it must be learned hard. But it must be learned even harder if it is not inborn trait as a prominent philosopher of Enlightenment era John Locke believed. Thus, altruism is a learned trait in any case and every generation should start from scratch.

This was a real problem for communists and the Nazis that tried unsuccessfully to build such societies in the past using so-called social engineering. In this respect, there are three conditions to be met to create and sustain an altruistic society.

Firstly, since humans are born as egoists, every generation should be coerced to go through the same forceful altruistic instructions (upbringing, education and training) in order to produce new altruists.

Secondly, this altruistic learning routines should be constantly reinforced all your life; otherwise, the learned altruism will be gradually dissolved exposing inborn egoism.

And finally, the hardest thing to achieve is that the learned altruistic experience must not contradict reality. In other words, if a learned altruist realizes that the teachers and most of the people around are egoistic anyway; that the whole scheme is a fantasy or fraud, such altruist will flip back into an egoist sooner or later.

So, an altruistic society is a product of a human fantasy called social engineering. It is doubtful that such society will reproduce enough learned altruists to hold up the avalanche of egoists born into this world every day. But a society that consists entirely of learned altruists is even further away from reality. Such society is Utopia that could be constructed only theoretically in a human mind. It is another fallacy about altruism.

Such artificial entity as altruistic society is self-defeating because one of its goals is to achieve economic equality. Imagine one altruist voluntarily gives to another altruist, and another and another. He does not know if anyone reciprocates or when. If he feels harmed or cheated, he will stop giving. As a result of this random and chaotic process, the cheaters will get more, and the honest ones will get less. What a ridiculous paradox: *an altruistic society breeds inequality* defeating the very purpose of altruism.

Thus, it cannot function properly in reality without coercion. To motivate and avoid inequality created by altruism, any *altruistic society* must resort to *mandatory withdrawal and arbitrary redistribution*, which must be brutally enforced by a *totalitarian authority*. And here is where the LFO altruism and totalitarianism are happily married.

Like the AIDS virus cannot live outside of a human body, an altruistic society cannot exist outside of a human mind. Reality kills it fast.

This reality was demonstrated in the past by the failed attempts to build altruistic communes in the US. Make a note: all of them were based on socialist principles—*altruism and socialism always come in one package.*

Look at Altruria, a short-lived small Utopian commune (about 30 learned altruists) organized by a Unitarian minister on Christian socialist principles in October 1894 near Santa Rosa, in Sonoma County, California. Similar communes were created also near San Francisco and Los Angeles. They kept orchards and gardens and sold their produce to support themselves. Altruria struggled for only two months and soon faced bankruptcy due to poor management and lack of funds. By 1986, they abandoned all their locations unable to support themselves—fantasy has met a real world.

Llano Del Rio was another altruistic commune appeared at what is now Llano, California in 1915. It was organized by a socialist lawyer Job Harriman on socialist principles of "equal ownership, equal wage, and equal social opportunities". The goal was to build an egalitarian, socialist society to transform capitalism from within. They built paint and print shops; grew corn and grain; and had poultry yard and fish hatchery, mostly for internal consumption. In their own school, their children were indoctrinated with socialist values. The commune was also short-lived and filed for bankruptcy in 1918. It quickly destructed itself due to a power struggle; authoritarian management; absence of democracy; false expectations; low wages; financial difficulties; rigid enforcement of altruistic equality and...defections of disappointed members to the capitalist surrounding paying higher wages. Here is why the socialists want to destroy capitalism so desperately. Competition with more prosperous capitalism kills them fast.

But the most notorious case is a utopian altruistic commune founded by a member of the communist party USA James Warren Jones in Guyana. Jim Jones believed that the only way to build socialism in the capitalist America was through religion. And he established his own church People's Temple to use religion for preaching another religion—Marxism and

Soviet style communism. His goal was to bring enlightenment (socialism) to those who were "drugged with the opiate of religion and capitalism". Among his idols were Vladimir Lenin, Joseph Stalin and Mao Tse-tung. A hard-core communist, he even broke with the Communist party USA for being critical of Joseph Stalin and socialism in the USSR.

In 1974, he established a utopian, socialist agrarian commune named after himself as Jonestown. Here in Guyana jungles, the members raised animals and vegetables for internal consumption on a rented plot. The goal was to establish an *altruistic*, benevolent model of *communist* community.

The commune imitated the social structure of the socialist states like USSR, Communist China and North Korea. Everything was owned in common; peoples lived altruistically for others under authoritarian rules; armed guards did not permit anybody to leave the commune; the members were deprived of elementary human rights and suffered from substandard living conditions; they were physically, emotionally and sexually abused—the conditions resembled those at hard-labor camps of the Soviet GULAG.

Due to escaped defectors, rumors about people held against their will at the commune reached the US. But when a US congressmen and the NBC TV crew visited the commune to investigate, they were killed by the Jones's henchmen on November 18, 1978. Later the same day more than 900 members of the commune and their children were found dead from cyanide poisoning; some were shot, including Jones. Jones called it a "revolutionary suicide." So, as Altruria and Llano Del Rio before it, the Jonestown socialist, altruistic experiment was also short-lived, except that hundreds were found dead.

However, the final guilty verdict was returned after the devastating fiasco of the grandiose, bloody, altruistic experiments in the USSR and other communist countries, except that millions were found dead.

A society based on learned altruism never worked; it does not work today; and it will never work in the future. Altruism is a learned trait and cannot be inherited.

The communists in the USSR and other communist countries were supposed to graduate hundreds of millions of altruists over the years. Where are all of them now? Russian and other "altruists" embraced self-interest and self-reliance virtually overnight.

What do Altruists and One-Ear Cows have in Common?

So, what choice is left for the proponents of altruistic societies? If the learned altruism is impotent to build one, then inborn altruism may accomplish that! The inborn altruists can reproduce themselves without life-long learning. The idea is that the government should subject many generations to vigorous altruistic training until altruists start giving birth to altruists. Eventually, the entire society will consist only of altruists. Altruism will become a natural, inborn human trait and people will get rid of egoism permanently and for all. That is the reason why the proponents of altruism have been trying to prove so desperately that altruistic genes exist.

To breed altruists! What an arrogant idea! Heredity is one of the most genius inventions created by Nature. Can the most hidden genetic secret guarded by Nature over millions of years be manipulated by learning? Can a learned trait be relatively quickly turned into inborn traits skipping the scrutiny of Nature? And the most horrific question: can a trait required by others be permanently installed in others through forced learning—the dream of socialists?

Here is a clever verbal exchange that shows that this idea is absolute absurdity. The exchange took place at a conference in the former USSR in the 1950s between biologist Trofim Lysenko (a staunch advocate of the government-supported but later discredited "learned heredity" theory) and a skeptic, the famous physicist, a Nobel-prize winner Lev Landau.

Lysenko: "If we subject the seeds of wheat to freezing; do the same to the next generation of seeds; and repeat it many times, then the wheat will eventually become frost-resistant and produce frost-resistant seeds."

Landau: "Wait a minute! Are you saying that if we cut off one ear from a cow, and will do the same to her off-springs, then the future generations of cows will eventually start giving birth to one-ear cows?

Lysenko: "Yes, of course."

Landau: "Then, how can you explain the birth of virgins?"

Lysenko: (Dead silence).

So, what do inborn altruists and one-ear cows have in common? The chance to give birth to one of them is about the same—zero.

Chapter 4
NATURE VS. NURTURE

THE DEBATE: NATURE VS. NURTURE

Why didn't I Become a Thief?

I have always been wondering about my childhood and teen years. Why did I become an engineer and a scientist? Why didn't I become a thief or a burglar when I was a kid? Why didn't I do time in a colony for delinquent juveniles or in prison when I was a teen as most of my playmates?

It was 1944 and the bloody war was still raging on. My parents returned to Kiev (Ukraine), the city where I was born. It was just liberated from Germans, and the ruins were everywhere. My playmates from a shabby, dirty apartment building where we lived were children of war. Most of them were fatherless. Always hungry, they were wild, ruthless and merciless creatures. We played together, and we fought each other to establish the hierarchy. There were some older kids, and they ruled.

They were bad boys, familiar with prison life and criminal world. They were involved in thievery and burglary. Some of them were fresh from prison; others were on the road leading there. Some were thought to be killers. Sometimes, the bad boys organized us as a gang to wage wars against other gangs around the block. Also, they told us stories about "glorious" world of thieves, their customs and laws. They were not stupid, and their world was not wrong. They were just different, and their laws were much simpler. What can I say; I was growing up in a very bad surrounding (*Environment* as they call it now).

Some bad kids struggled desperately to rehabilitate themselves in better surroundings. They returned to school or got jobs; married and had kids. But not for long, like my cousin's husband Tim who was in and out of prison until he died fairly young. "*A bad seed*," my mother used to say about him, meaning that he would grow up bad no matter what. It seemed to me at that time that my mother was right: *Good Environment was too weak to influence Bad Seeds (human nature)*.

But some seemingly good kids of my age and older were lured into that "glorious" life; became school dropouts and eventually criminals. Their young lives were ruined, and some lives were lost. Bad Environment! It was overwhelming and powerful: it turned a good person into a bad person. In other words, *Bad Environment was stronger than Good Seeds.*

Yet, some kids (including me) resisted to that temptation. I played soccer with the bad boys; I sang prison songs with them, but I did not go "on a deal" with them. My parents were undereducated and poor. They were both working hard and come home late and exhausted. I was one on one with this relentless, destructive environment. But I wanted to go to school, to study, to learn and become an engineer or a scientist.

We had no books at home; I was buying thin soft-covered booklets of a popular-science series about the origin of life, cosmos, animals, and other "ridiculous" stuff. Of course, mom did not know where my school-lunch money went and why I was always hungry after school and thin. Some powerful force inside was dragging me on that off-beat path until...I really became a scientist. Obviously, I was a good seed (at least my wife said so). Now, it became confusing: *bad Environment was powerless to corrupt a good Seed.*

More and more puzzling and confusing stories emerged about hard criminals who did turn their lives around influenced by a good environment, religion, ideology, near-death experience, etc. Or about people who were born and raised in a very good environment by educated parents and in loving families, but selected life outside of the society and became criminals.

Environment or Human Nature! Who cares?

As I walked through life, I tried to sort these stories out. I changed my mind several times with each new story I heard from people or read in newspapers. My motivation was to make sense of my life. Why was I spared from becoming a criminal? What spared me from wasting my life? What is the purpose of my life then?

Here is the problem (to make it visual): you have soil (Environment); you sow a seed (inborn human character) and you grow a plant (Person's behavior).

Environment may be bad (B) like a prison or good (G) like a normal family, school, etc. Seeds also may be bad like my cousin's husband Tim or good like me. The resulting person's behaviors may be bad or good either. For example, if you take a bad soil and sow a bad seed in it, you will grow a bad plant: B + B = B. Simple as that.

But here is my life. Philosophically, it squeezed into one short formula: B + G = G meaning that a bad soil did not prevent a good seed from growing into a good plant. How could it be?

Probability! My life was probably a truly rare case because I was obviously an extremely good seed. This made me feel like a hero and sometimes brag about it.

Still, my assumption that the environment and seeds are either good or bad was too primitive. In real life, there are innumerous shades between black and white. In fact, if 100 intermediate grades of environment interact with 100 intermediate grades of seeds, it may produce up to 10,000 combinations and, thus, corresponding results (behaviors). But 1,000 grades may produce a staggering 1,000,000 behaviors! No wonder that the badness or the goodness of each person's behavior is unique.

This means that I created a myth in my mind about my "heroic" life. The reason I became a good person might not be because I was extremely good seed but because the environment was not extremely bad. In fact, I was not forced to steal by bad kids (I was probably not good at such things). Also, I did not grow in a colony or a prison.

Well, at that time, I have not found an answer why I didn't become a criminal. Maybe, both environment and human nature turned me into a person I have become...

What a useless mental exercise performed at a wrong time and a wrong place! Environment or human Nature! Who cares about such insignificant things when people around me were thinking about more serious things—mostly how to put bread on the table for their families and survive?

Little I knew at that time that this question was at the center of a fierce, millennium-long philosophical, academic debate and uncompromised struggle for human souls. I did not even suspect that the innocent facade of this abstract, academic debate hid a sobering, grim and bloody reality; that almost every human being on this planet has been either an involuntary participant or a victim of this debate.

Debate or Bloody Nightmare?

I did not become a victim of this debate because I kept my mouth shut. You see, the very thought that human nature is responsible for your behavior was dangerous—it was outright criminal in the eyes of the communist authorities.

We were taught that the Marxist-Leninist's teaching was supposed to uproot any vices our parents might have as remnants of the capitalist's past. But the next generation (like me) was not supposed to have those vices and wrong ideas. I was supposed to grow up as a "Soviet Man," a new, superior human being Nature has never seen before.

We were taught that Man was born with "a clean mind," and it was the duty of the socialist state to fill it with the right ideas and values. We were supposed to think as we were taught—*to think as others*. We were supposed to pass the superior qualities of the "Soviet Man" to the next generation. If you still have those vices, you obviously picked them up from the enemies of the state. Therefore you have to be reeducated in a hard-labor camp. This was the main reason why the science of genetics was banned in the USSR; it was associated with heredity and could contradict the official Marxist view point.

Later I found out that the "clean-mind" concept was the basis of the so-called "Nurture" theory innocently formulated by the thinkers of the Enlightenment era (John Locke, Claude-Adrian Helvétius and others) in the 17th and 18th centuries. And after centuries of academic debates, the theory was finally put into practice in the 20th century. Socialists (Russian communists, Italian fascists and German Nazis) utilized it to make critical contributions to their theories of a "New Man."

As Richard Pipes[1] writes: "The communist state established by Lenin in Russia in 1917 was a grandiose experiment in public education undertaken on Helvétius model for the purpose of creating an entirely new type of human being, one rid of vices, including acquisitiveness."

As a survivor of this socialist experiment, I remember mandatory government (Marxist-Leninist) educational courses that were taught (nurtured) at kindergartens, schools and colleges. While such indoctrination continued through your entire life, not a shred of information was allowed to leak outside of the government sources. We were taught to have no desire for material things; any greed or envy; to become selfless altruists caring only for others (for Marxist ideology and the Government). As a tiny neuron in a gigantic brain, your only function was to carry out any orders from the brain.

Those who received low grades or failed these Marxist's educational courses were simply disposed—millions of them disappeared. The survivors were pretenders or those who passed the tests. In fact, I would call this practice an *ideological form of Eugenics* although such term does not exist.

Think about that. The original Eugenics theory was introduced by English scientist Sir Francis Galton in the 19th century. Although the term has many meanings now, the original one may be reduced to a simple question: who deserve to live on the planet Earth? And the original answer was biological in nature—people of good physical and mental health, and higher than average abilities. But look what the Russian socialists have done: they said that only those who believe in the Marxist-Leninist theory deserve to live. Practiced by socialists, this was a horrific ideological form of Eugenics to purify human race ideologically according to their Marxist-Leninist theory. (This is similar to a religious form of Eugenics the radical Islamists practice today).

And it worked: all people around you claimed that they were the believers in Marxism-Leninism; they spoke alike and seemingly thought alike. However, they were still full of pernicious vices, just hid them. They were craving secretly for material things; stealing your possessions and ideas; they were full of envy; they were greedy, status-seeking and jealous as Nature intended them to be at birth. And the bright image of the "Soviet Superman" was crumbling despite the indoctrination.

People were turning into cynics motivated only by their self-interest and acting accordingly when nobody was watching. No wonder that, after the collapse of the Soviet Union, it took only a couple of years for Nature to reclaim the egoistic souls of those phony altruists forcibly nurtured to do the opposite for 70 years. People returned to their natural disposition (egoism) with such an ease. How superficial and impotent indoctrination (nurture) is if it contradicts reality and human nature!

The Nazis, national socialists, pursued the same goal: to create an altruistic society where every one cares only about others (about the Nazis ideology). Using the same violent indoctrination methods as the communists did, they were trying to create a new, superior "Arian Man." They also believed that the superior qualities of the German race could be propagated through heredity (blood). But they employed a different form of Eugenics, racial Eugenics—getting rid of people who could taint German blood and interfere with the creation of a pure, superior Arian race.

It worked too when Hitler's war machine crashed one nation after another reinforcing the image of a German soldier as a superior human being. But this image quickly crumbled when it was subjected to a real test on the Eastern (Russian) front. Again, indoctrination (nurture) contradicted reality: an inferior race was winning.

By the way, it is not surprising to see Russian socialists/communists and German national socialists on the same page of history. No wonder, why the documentaries exposing Nazi ideology were forbidden in the USSR—there were so many striking similarities with the communist ideology.

Communism and Nazism are twin-brothers who grew up together, but became estranged fighting for the inheritance of their parents Socialism.

History of the Debate
　　Those were my naive thoughts at that time, the time when access to information was a dangerous game. But time is flying fast. All of a sudden, I found myself on the other side of the planet with a wealth of information at my disposal. One day searching the Internet, I stumbled over a strange domain Nature vs. Nurture.

　　To my great delight, it was a debate between philosophers and scientists of many disciplines (psychology, sociology, sociobiology, anthropology, etc) about what is the main factor in human development: heredity/human genes (Nature) or environmental factors of the upbringings (Nurture or Environment).

　　The history of the debate has just blown me away. It was like a bloody war between human nature and environment waged on the fields of a human mind. It reminded me a blind Man walking on a millennium-long dangerous road in search of the truth and enlightenment.

　　On one side of the debate[1] was ancient and medieval traditional thinking prevailed in the Western civilization: Man is made up of body and soul. The soul is filled with inborn ideas and (natural) values implanted in it at birth. Human nature/character is fixed and is solely responsible for human behavior. In other words, if Man is born bad, bad he will remain. This idea was a predecessor of the *Nature theory*.

　　However, the opposite school of thoughts (a predecessor of the *Nurture theory*) claimed that there was no inborn human nature; that human intellect at birth is blank as a *"tabula rasa"* (clean slate, in Latin); and that all knowledge is attained by Man through the senses of perception, which govern Man's behavior. These ideas could be traced back to both ancient time (Aristotle) and medieval time (13th century Italian priest St. Thomas Aquinas[2]).

The phrase Nature vs. Nurture first appeared in a manuscript titled Silence. It was discovered in 1911 but written in 13th century France by an unknown writer Heldriss of Cornwell[3]. This philosophical novel framed the debate that has been raging ever since[4]. It is a story about a young woman, named Silence who was raised as a boy. Heldriss described two allegoric characters Nature (heredity) and Nurture (environment, upbringing, education, life experience) who debated fiercely for her loyalty and, eventually, who is the true author of a person. Ahead of his time, Heldriss recognized that both the environment (Nurture) and character (Nature) could influence human behavior, the idea that received confirmations only by the end of the 20th century.

At the end of 17th century, John Locke, a prominent English philosopher of the Enlightenment era, has laid the foundation for the Nurture theory. He flatly denied the existence of inborn ideas (human nature) and believed that human behavior is shaped only by environment[5].

Influenced by John Locke, French philosopher Claude-Adrian Helvétius went even further reinforcing the Nurture theory[6]. But he carried the Locke theory to its extremes. He believed that all human being had equal mental capacity and that their behavior can be (and should be) properly molded by the government through mandatory instructions and education. Thus, Helvétius was the father of so-called "social engineering" notoriously put into practice in the 20th century.

The Nurture theory was not seriously challenged after Locke although some philosophers (like the 18th century French philosopher Denis Dederot) strongly opposed it and believed in heredity; and although the 19th century English scientist Sir Francis Galton[7] came independently to the same conclusions as Heldriss of Cornwell more than 600 years before him.

In the 19th century, the Nurture theory was tragically embraced by Marxist and socialist ideologues. It entered the 20th century with a bang: Russian communists and German national-socialists put it into practice in the bloodiest human experiment in human history. In modern days, the Nurture theory received its continuation in the works of an influential American psychologist B. F. Skinner[8] at Harvard University.

The first serious cracks in its foundation appeared when a psychologist at Harvard University E.O. Wilson introduced the Nature theory and the concept of Sociobiology in 1975. The concept[9] applied Darwin's evolution theory to human behavior and viewed many human emotions, thoughts and social behaviors as genetically inherited and fixed. Human beings are seen as another species of animals and part of Nature.

The Nature theory has always been viewed as politically incorrect and treated with hostility and indignation by liberal and left-leaning establishment, media and academia. No wonder, the Nature theory contradicts Marxist understanding of a human nature as malleable. They claim that the Nature theory has to be wrong because it makes people believe that there are genes responsible for human IQ, aggression, greed, egoism or homosexuality. They fear that it may undermine their political agenda.

Unfortunately, the Nurture theory that denies the existence of human nature still dominates the thoughts of liberal and left-leaning academia despite the failure of the communist and Nazi ideologies. Neither the advances in genetics nor better understanding of heredity made it disappear also. Although researchers all around the world believe now that both human nature and environment may play roles in human behavior and search for genes responsible for certain behavioral traits, the Nurture theory stubbornly defies reality.

CAN SOCIALISM CHANGE HUMAN NATURE?

Inborn traits or learned traits? That's the question!
Despite the catastrophic consequences of practical implementation of the Nurture theory that denies the existence of the inborn traits, the theory still dominates the thoughts and practices of academia, media, Hollywood and the governments. Sinister echo of Nature vs. Nurture debate still resonates in people's lives.

Do you remember a popular movie Trading Places (1983) starring Eddie Murphy (Billy Ray Valentine) and Dan Aykroyd (Louis Winthorpe III)? It is easy to notice that the authors are propagating a progressive agenda (rich vs. poor; racial and economic equality; and exposure of greedy capitalism).

But entertainment is not the only thing on the author's mind in this funny comedy. What is less noticeable how the Hollywood leftists are involved in the debate Nature vs. Nurture.

A *disgusting*, grouchy owner of a prestigious brokerage firm Mortimer Duke believes that human character is determined at birth by Nature, while his *sympathetic* brother Randolph believes that human behavior is a product of Nurture (environment). And the authors set the stage for a collision between Nature and Nurture? Who do you think will triumph considering ideological orientation of the authors?

Of course, environment! Billy Ray Valentine—a poorly educated and ill-mannered black street-hustler wins with his hands down! After being placed in a good environment by the whim of two brothers, the poor beggar turns into a dignified and successful manager of this brokerage firm, just over night. At the same time, Louis Winthorpe III, a highly educated and classy manager replaced by Billy, becomes a petty thief living at the expense of a prostitute.

The movie was made in the best traditions of the left-wing progressive ideology and in the spirit of Helvétius. It illustrates that a beggar and Harvard graduate possess equal mental capacity; that human character or behavior depend only on environment and can be molded by others. That is how trained Hollywood progressive S.E.A.L.s are conducting covert operations behind the capitalist enemy's lines. Although the story is disguised as an innocent attempt to make the film funny and make money, it still serves its ideological purpose, even if it flies in the face of reality.

Here is the reality! Remember a sensational story about Norman Kingsley Mailer, a famous American progressive writer, and his protégée? Mailer helped a notorious murderer to start literary career; got him out of prison; and placed him in a good environment. Ideologically left-leaning Mailer believed that the killer would turn into a civilized man (like Eddie Murphy in Trading Places), but the guy killed again within months from being released—a civilized sugar coating (the learned behavior) did not change the murder-provoking inborn traits hidden underneath.

William Shakespeare put it bluntly: *"Man evil manners live in brass; their virtues we write in water."* Over the years, psychologists found hundreds of "evil manners and virtues" that shape human behavior. But the focus of the debate raging for centuries has always been on two types of human traits (features of a character): inborn (innate) vs. learned traits. To be or not to be is the eternal question asked by Shakespeare hundreds of years ago. Inborn trait or learned trait is the question of the same philosophical magnitude.

Learned traits are acquired through education, life experience and interactions with other people and environment. Think about selflessness, kindness, honesty, humor, to name a few. The learned traits have been known since Man learned to understand abstract concepts and found ingenious ways to pass their knowledge and experience to other people. Due to the achievements in science, technology and medicine, the environment became less hostile to Man, but more complex. Behavior of modern humans is influenced decreasingly less by climate changes and predators, but increasingly more by culture, education and learning. They are influenced not only by the people next to them, but by those who are thousands of miles away or lived thousands of years ago.

Inborn (innate) traits are gained through heredity at birth and represent human nature or character. The existence of inborn traits has been denied by philosophers and behavioral scientists for centuries. But what are those traits if their existence is denied?

Here is a deal: if a person's trait causes a shameful behavior that is encouraged by no one; if it is harmful to, rejected and condemned by every one—this is an inborn trait, no questions about it. Think about envy, jealousy, greed, egoism, aggression, acquisitiveness and many others.

The most controversial points of the debate are about the inborn, inherited traits. Do the inborn traits exist? If they do exist, who they are inherited from? Are they fixed and unchanged since the primordial time? What are those traits? Do they still shape the behavior of modern people? Have they been replaced with the learned traits that represent civilized, humane behavior by now? Let's apply common sense in answering those questions.

Do the Inborn Traits Really Exist?

It is estimated that modern humans (Homo sapiens) exist for about 200,000 years. Other homo species closely related to them are about 2.3-2.4 million years old.[11]

If you think about a savage, you think about aggression, not a sense of humor. In the same token, envy, jealousy, greed, acquisitiveness and other traits may be traced way back to homo species, Neanderthals and pre-Columbus Indians. Those traits were gradually evolved as a response to and were perfected by the natural environment (hostile elements; dangerous predators; competition with animals and other homo species for resources). Those traits were passed to countless generations to increase their chances to survive and reproduce.

We do not teach our kids to kill, steal or envy; and be egoists, greedy, stingy or acquisitive. We teach them just the opposite. But this is out of our control sometimes; those stubborn traits are still there. If they are not inborn and inherited from our ancestors, where they came from despite centuries of enlightenment, education and indoctrination?

If the recorded modern human history (about 6,000 years) had been an equivalent of a human life span (about 70 years), then modern Man would have been just about 2-month old baby in comparison with the Homo species that existed for 2.4 million years. Thus, most of the traits inherited from our savaged ancestors are likely to remain intact for such a short period. They are still present and fixed permanently in modern humans. Is the anger of a modern human different from the anger of a savage? Both will kill in anger. Nature has gauged anger and other inborn traits into a human nature (genome) like running water gauges into a granite rock.

Although the inborn traits have been very beneficial for animals and primordial humans, they are considered ugly, undesirable and uncivilized by modern Man. A sugar coating on top of a pill hides its bitter taste and makes it easy to swallow. But it does not replace its content. A learned trait does the same thing. It serves as an idealistic sugar coating that covers an inborn trait, but it does not replace or change it. An inborn trait is hidden underneath of a corresponding civilized learned trait gained by Man after birth: egoism—under altruism; anger—under gentleness; greed—under generosity. Under stress, a powerful inborn instinct bursts through a thin sugar coating and modern Man behaves as a savage or an animal. This was evident to Charles Darwin himself who acknowledged in Descent of Man (1871) that "... man with all his noble qualities, still bears in his bodily frame the indelible stamp of his lowly origin."

If modern scientists deny the existence of inherited human traits, let's hear what the ancient people said about that. Our ancestors knew how to build the Pyramids; they knew about astronomy and the planets before the telescope was invented; and they knew about inherited and learned human traits too.

In fact, their messages are in the Hebrew Bible! Just read the Ten Commandments written 3,500 years ago! The ancient people knew then that a human mind had always been filled with envy, hate, anger, greed, acquisitiveness, selfishness, vanity, lust and many others inborn traits. Surprise! You can recognize many of them in animals and people today, as well.

In fact, Roderick C. Meridith[10] explains that the goal of the Ten Commandments revealed to Moses by God is to give an opportunity to choose between Good and Evil. Good is good human virtues to be learned through God's wisdom. And Evil is bad human weaknesses entrenched in every human soul from birth. In other words, Good means learned traits, which are good, and Evil means inborn traits, which are bad. The goal is to replace the bad, inborn traits with the good, learned traits.

So, the ancient people gave us, the civilized humans, 3,500 years to replace the bad, undesirable inborn traits with the good, desirable learned ones. Why, in the world, haven't we learned how to do it by now? Are we so stupid? Of course, not! Was the learning period not sufficient? For God's sake, no! Man was learning these educational courses for several thousand semesters—every year, no summer breaks!

So what is the problem? The problem arises when Man starts messing with human nature. *Human nature is given us by Nature and can be changed only by Nature.*

"Not true!" socialists say. "People were taught wrong way. Socialist ideals can change and improve human nature for the better." Is that so? Let's see if this is true.

Did Socialists Improve Human Nature?

These ugly inborn traits! We can find the most familiar and notorious of them in the Ten Commandments of the book of Exodus[12], namely in Commandments # 6 through #10. They are easy to recognize because they may be traced to animals and our savage ancestors. Let's see how the socialists suppressed and rejuvenated a human nature for the better in the communist Russia.

Commandments #6: "Thou shalt not kill (murder)." Murdering (intentional killing) has always been a way of life in animals. It was practiced also by Homo species millions of years ago as well as savage tribes in Africa and pre-Columbus America thousands of years ago. And murder is still the way of life in our civilized society also (homicides, massacres, genocides, wars) despite millenniums-long education. The timeless human traits that compel Man to murder are *the inborn traits*. Man kills out of *Envy, Hate, Anger, Jealousy (*and sometimes…for a pair of expensive sneakers on the Southside of Chicago).

The socialists claimed that they suppressed and rejuvenated those murder-provoking inborn traits. But in reality, the Soviet people still harbored hate and anger; envy and jealousy as every human being on Earth. Crime statistics were the state secret because homicide was the fact of everyday life in the USSR. The socialist utopia did not end the practice of murdering people. Moreover, the communists (as well as the national socialists, the Nazi) turned murdering people into a policy instrument.

Animals kill on an individual basis because of predation (it has to eat) and rarely because of rivalry (it has to mate and own its territory); our savage ancestors killed individuals or small group of people out of hate, anger, envy or jealousy. But look what the socialists did! They killed people by millions for not believing in their theories; for being religious; or belonging to a "wrong" nationality.

Just recall numerous political purges in the USSR (millions were shot to death); genocide in the Soviet Ukraine during the communist-made famine (millions were starved to death); horrific GULAG hard-labor camps (millions were worked out to death). And do not forget to add the Holocaust of Jews in Germany and Europe perpetrated by the National Socialists (millions were burnt in crematoriums). In Eastern Europe, China, Vietnam, Cambodia, or Cuba—everywhere the socialists played out the same murderous scenario. And on top of it, the horrific WWII concocted by Russian and German socialists.

Overall, socialists butchered more than a hundred million people in the 20th century—the bloodiest century in human history. This appalling slaughter could not be accomplished without turning millions of otherwise normal people into willing accomplices, bloody sadists and murderers.

Sometimes, I wonder why the wise Nature put up with a structure of a human society—the murderous socialist system. What is the hidden purpose of allowing it to exist even for a minute? Well, the effective reduction of overpopulation, I guess. No system in the history of mankind does it better!

Socialists *distorted and mutilated human nature* on a scale never seen before by tearing down the boarded doors leading to the darkest, murderous corners of a human nature.

Commandments #7: "Thou shalt not commit adultery." Among animal species, males are often polygamous (they mate with multiple females). Monogamous relationships are very rare in animals; they were probably rare in Homo species because they did not appear to be always advantageous for procreation. How many swans we see around and how many rats? The basic drive is to insure that the genetic codes of individuals survive their death and are transferred to new generations. In fact, according to summer 1994 Times magazine's cover story, 87% of known 1154 human societies allow multiple wives. So, adultery in a civilized, monogamous society is a recurrence of the same inborn genetic drive, which is very much alive and wide spread. It manifests itself in *inborn traits* such as *Lust, Unfaithfulness and Promiscuousness* very well known to everyone (especially Hollywood stars, politicians and long-distance truck drivers).

"Not in a socialist state," the socialists object. "Socialist ideals radically changed the relationships between men and women. People were punished by the state for adultery, which was considered as a betrayal of socialist ideals. The adulterers usually lost their status, positions or jobs."

True, some ordinary philanderers were punished, but not the communist party leaders and the members of the party nomenclature. Married Lenin caught syphilis from prostitutes; Stalin, Khrushchev, Brezhnev and other staunched, hard-nosed communists were notorious adulterers. Lavrenti Beria (the chief of the secret police under Stalin) used to kidnap good-looking women from the streets of Moscow. As a result, adulterous behavior of ordinary Soviet people as well as the rate of divorce turned for the worse due to hypocrisy of those who preached the socialists ideals.

A strong family is a guarantee of societal stability. Adultery leads to break-down of a family and thus, to disintegration of a society. That is what our domestic progressives and socialists dream about—disintegration of the capitalist society. Then, everything that facilitates adultery is welcomed, especially pornography, sex and violence promoted by Hollywood, the faithful vanguard of the progressive movement.

Socialists *corrupt human nature* turning sacred monogamy cherished by civilized human beings into travesty.

Commandments #8:" Thou shalt not steal." Animals do not miss an opportunity to take a kill away from another animal to survive and propagate. Our ancestors did the same for thousands of years. It was natural for them, but modern Man calls it stealing now that is taking something that is not yours. So, stealing takes place only where there is yours and mine; where there is the right to possess property. For thousands of years, people are taught that the right way to acquire property was by a free gift or honest labor. Then, why are thievery and robbery problems still entrenched in the modern human society regardless of punishment? Why did cheating become a way of life at schools, colleges and businesses as well as in politics?

"Who cheats? Just, about everyone if the stakes are right... Cheating is a primordial economic act: getting more for less," believes Harvard economist Steven Levitt in his book Freakonomics[13]. So, the only difference between stealing and cheating is that stealing is getting something for free, while cheating is getting for less. Stealing can be traced to such inborn traits as *Envy:* I want what you have and I will get it either by hook (robbery) or crook (thievery). Cheating can be traced to *Laziness:* why to work hard if I can get it by working less?

"Wait a minute, stealing is a trademark of capitalism driven by greed and possession of private property!" say socialists. "Socialism brings different relationships between people because there is no private property; no yours and mine; everything is owned in common. Who will steal from yourself if everything *belongs to you?*"

Oh, come on! Thievery was the way of life in the USSR. The vast majority of the population was stealing everything imaginable on an unimaginable scale. Peasants were stealing food produce from collective farms; workers—household goods from factories; healthcare providers—medicine from hospitals. Ironically, they were not stealing from themselves, and they did not call it stealing; they were taking what *belonged to them*. Just the opposite, they believed that the Government was stealing the fruits of their labor. Driven by poverty and deprivation of every necessity, people were confused about what was yours and what was mine; they could not tell the difference between good and bad, as well.

Socialists *abused human nature* turning the entire society into pathological petty-thieves.

Commandments #9: "Thou shalt not bear false witness against thy neighbor." This commandment exposes lies; vanity (to make others to believe in your inflated importance); and slander (a lie invented and spread with intent to harm others). These traits can be traced back to animals and our ancient ancestors. In fact, when a predator hides behind rocks or uses camouflage (disguise) to ambush its prey, this act of deception is an animal's way of lying. When a peacock spreads its fabulous tail to attract a female, this showoff act is similar to vanity. (No wonder vanity is associated with a peacock image). When a crow mimics a barking dog (probably to scare birds into leaving their nests and their young), this is an animal's way of slandering dogs. In any case, all species (especially modern humans) do it to get ahead at the expense of others. So, what makes people untruthful; full of vanity or conceit? Or to slander, slur, smear, vilify or defame other people? Heredity! Many of us still harbor these *inborn traits* no matter how hard we try to discredit them and hide deep inside. Like a genie corked inside the bottle, they are waiting for a chance to be released.

And the bottle was uncorked by socialists. They turned USSR into a police state where almost every one became an informer and a false witness against his neighbor. People became suspicious and distrustful of each other. Here is a joke that characterizes atmosphere in the socialist state.

"What did they put you away for?" an inmate asks his cellmate.

"Just for laziness! I and my friend were shooting anti-government jokes. It was late when I came home; so I decided to report my friend in the morning. But in the morning, they took me away."

The socialist ideals cannot exist without lies; the history of the USSR is the most falsified document in the recorded human history. They promised factories to workers; land to peasants; and freedom to people—they lied. They claimed that they created the most prosperous society on Earth—they lied too: people lived in poverty. They claimed that they created a society of free people although millions were rotting in the Siberian hard-labor camps. Their claim that the socialist society is the Paradise was pure vanity.

The socialists *suppressed* a diverse *human nature* trying to mold it so that all people are thinking the same way as dictated by the Government. Those who did not conform were slandered, smeared, vilified and defamed as the enemy of the people, foreign spies or simply anti-Soviet agitators. No one was spared from slander, persecution and GULAG: political opposition; non-conformist intellectuals; starving, revolting peasants; striking factory workers; free-thinking poets, writers and musicians; unorthodox scientists; non-reliable segments of non-Russian population.

Socialists *perverted human nature* to the extent that people acquired a permanent, psychotic guard against saying what they think, while slander, lie and betrayal became the way of everyday life in the USSR.

Commandments #10: "Thou shalt not covet (desire)." This is a warning against desires to possess neighbor's wife, house, status, talent, etc. This is notorious *Envy*, one of the most prominent features of animal and human natures. Are you watching the Animal Planet on TV? Watch how male lions desire and battle for the neighbor's territory and females. Why? It is because their own successful survival and reproduction depends on "neighbor's house and wives." Human ancestors did the same. Beside *Envy*, these behaviors can be traced to such *inborn traits* as *Acquisitiveness, Avarice, Selfishness* and *Greed*. In modern societies, they result in a fierce competition to get ahead in status, position, power and resources; and in accumulation of more and more material things.

"Those ugly traits can exist only in a greedy capitalist society," cry socialists. "The socialist ideals are against envy, greed, desire for material things and other pernicious traits of a human nature."

Ironically, socialists thought that they would get rid of acquisitiveness and greed by leaving people without material things and making them dependant on the Government's handouts. But they suppressed human nature only temporarily—acquisitiveness and greed just went underground; people hid them silently inside and followed the rule: don't stick out. One of the most damaging consequences of messing with a human nature was that people perverted by the Government's handouts lost their free spirit of self-reliance, entrepreneurship and risk taking generously given to Man by Nature. They were stripped off their ability to act and make decisions on their own without a nod from above.

As for Envy, Nature has burned Envy into a hard rock of a human nature at birth and for life to prevent anyone from messing with it. Nevertheless, socialists managed to turn this relatively innocuous trait into one of the most destructive weapon in their arsenal. How did they "weaponize" envy? We will talk about it next.

In conclusions, socialists declared war on human nature that was perfected by Nature for millions of years. Claiming that it was full of pernicious vices and trying to mold it according to their socialist ideals, they were suppressing, distorting, corrupting, abusing and perverting human nature on a scale never seen before. In the process, they turned millions of otherwise normal people into bloody sadists and murderers. They turned the sacred and cherished monogamy into a mockery. They turned the entire society into uncontrolled cheaters and petty-thieves; into hypocrites speaking opposite to what they are thinking; into lying conformists, informers and slanderers. And most of all, they stripped people off their self-reliance, entrepreneurship, risk taking abilities; their ability to act freely and make decisions on their own.

In other words, socialists went against Nature: they accused human nature of pernicious vices and were trying to suppress or mold it. But they did not rejuvenate human nature; they perverted it! French philosopher of the 18th century Denis Dederot put it candidly: 'It is not human nature we should accuse, but the despicable conventions that perverted it."

HOW DID SOCIALISTS "WEAPONIZE" ENVY?

What is Envy?

Do you remember the movie "When Harry Met Sally?" There is a scene where Sally loudly fakes an orgasm at the table in a crowded cafeteria and a women sitting nearby asks a waiter: "Bring me what she is having!" It is a very funny joke because it implies sex. But it comes unnoticed that it also implies Envy. Envy is a complex, puzzling and indestructible emotion (some call it a trait of a human nature because it stays with you all your life).

What is Envy? Envy is "the desire to have for oneself something possessed by others." This is the definition given by the World English Dictionary. Since almost everything around us belongs to others nowadays, most of our desires may look like envy.

Envy was cultivated, encouraged and justified by Nature in animals and our ancestors for millions of years helping them to survive. If a sea gull catches a fish, scores of others want it for themselves and rush to take it away. It is Envy in animals, pure and simple. But it has a dual purpose: a fresh catch attracts other sea gulls to the area of good fortune. It encourages them to search harder in order to catch their own fish too. It is also caused by envy.

Are these behaviors deplorable or admirable? Neither, both are natural! Nature does not give the sea gulls a choice: rob others or work harder. It is an animal's nature. It is their way of life and their way to survive. Naturally, most of sea gulls have to work harder; robbing others cannot support everyone or for long.

Does it look familiar? Had Man gone far from animals, in this respect? Not really. Envy has been and remains one of the most prominent inborn traits in a human nature too. No matter how you call it emotion or trait, you have it from the birth and for the rest of your life.

If you rent an apartment, while your neighbor has a house, don't tell me that you do not envy. You do. If your neighbor goes to college, but you don't, you envy too. In a way, Envy is a desire to even the score with your neighbor, not the people you do not know. You are not burning from envy if some Joe Blow won the lottery; and you do not desire what Bill Gates possesses—both are not your neighbors. So, what's wrong with just a desire? Nothing wrong!

But Envy is not that simple. In Man's world, Envy is deplorable and shameful. It is not particularly flattering to hear that you are full of envy, and no one admits it in front of other people. But everyone harbors envy and tries to hide it deep inside because a stigma is attached to that trait. It is one of the "Seven Deadly Sins" in Catholic religion. Even if your Envy is innocent and does not harbor ill feelings, you will be guilty by association with those who take joy in the misfortune of others.

Usually, inborn traits are considered evil and have their noble antipodes (learned traits): Egoism—Altruism; Greed—Generosity; etc. I tried to find an antipode for Envy in Russian or English languages—there was none. I found only a Buddhist concept called *mudita*, which means to take joy in the good fortune of others. But this noble concept is not an exact antipode of Envy; otherwise, good will, kindness or generosity would be the antipodes of Envy too.

The absence of the antipode may mean that Envy is as universal and natural in humans as the desire to eat or drink. It may mean also that Envy is so indestructible, entrenched and irreplaceable that Man had given up his desire to replace it with something noble long ago.

I never admitted that I pursued my advanced degree out of envy because some of my colleagues-scientists got it. Honestly, it bothered me. If they can do it, why can't I do it too? And I did it no matter how hard it was. I didn't do any harm to anyone by doing that. Moreover, I helped many through my contribution to science. Still, I never confess that I did it out of envy until now. If asked, I used to say that I followed a good example; that I followed my dream. Why are we so ashamed to admit this? It is because Envy has two faces.

Two Faces of Envy

By the definition, envy consists of two parts: a desire and the object of this desire. The first part is not pernicious at all. My neighbor has a house, and I envy him because I want a house too. There is nothing wrong to have a desire. If you turn Envy into a dream; mobilize all your inner resources; work harder and eventually buy a house of your own, envy is rather positive trait of a human nature.

Moreover, Envy is a powerful driving force to make an enormous difference in your life and the lives of others. This is the force that motivates and inspires Man to get most of life; the force that propels Man to create, achieve and excel. Majority of the most spectacular Man's achievements is likely due to Envy—the desire to surpass your fellow-scientists, artists or actors; the desire to even the score with your neighbors, your countrymen or the entire world. In Russian culture, such envy is called "*white*" *Envy*.

But it is the second part of the definition of Envy that makes this trait so controversial, treacherous and dangerous. What is the object of your desire? Which house do you want? And how do you intend to get it?

If you are possessed with "white" Envy, you do not wish to see your neighbor's house on fire. If you want to build your own house as big as or bigger than your neighbor's, this is fine. You built it and elevated yourself to your neighbor's level.

Now, you are even and equal with your neighbor. And this is how "white" envy may reduce economic inequality. Although it cannot achieve full equality, still it tends to benefit others.

But what if you do not have enough patience and desire to work hard and wait until you do build your house? What if you want your neighbor's house?

Unlike animals, Man does have a choice. You may wish to burn your neighbor's house or to help others to take it away. Now, when your neighbor does not have a house any more, both of you are even and equal. You brought your neighbor down to your level, but you didn't even the score; you got even. In English culture, such envy is called *"green" Envy*. And this is the way how the *green Envy is helpful in achieving full economic Equality*.

The green Envy is deplorable and harmful trait of a human nature. It may manifest itself in whining, bitching, ill-wishing and back-stabbing. But a real danger is that Envy resides next door to its good pal *Hate*. If you cannot have your neighbor's house, then green *Envy* turns to *Hate* for help; and Hate always comes to the rescue and helps to burn your neighbor's house, no questions asked.

Envy is Weapon of Mass Destruction

As individuals, we envy people we know—our neighbors, friends and co-workers. Most of us try our best to even the score or surpass them, while some may resort to cowardly backstabbing to get ahead. This is a human nature; we and our ancestors have been born with it. Still, envy does not have enough destructive power to push a society off balance. Well, the envy energy of an individual is small, and each of us knows only a few people. Also, this energy is chaotically directed, dispersed and scattered around.

However, envy may push a society off balance if the envy energies of all individuals of a large group are combined and aimed in one direction. Then, envy becomes an enormous and immensely destructive force. Fortunately, this phenomenon never happens in Nature. It is foreign to a human nature also—one individual envies only one or several individuals whom they know. But socialists made masses of people envy a small group of people they do not know—they invented *class envy*. And here is how socialists insulted Nature and abused human nature.

Class envy is one of the most destructive forces employed by socialists because the entire society is loosely divided into two classes: "the haves" and "the have-nots." And here is how socialists "weaponize" envy—they fill it with hatred. Then, the envy energy of millions combined with hate is aimed in one direction. Now, it turns into a powerful laser beam, a tremendous damaging force. Now, it can be used as a weapon of mass destruction causing devastation that is difficult to predict and control.

That is what happened in Russia in 1917 where the socialists provoked the most destructive and bloody catastrophe in the 20th century. The envy of masses was combined with hate; then, this explosive mixture was ignited and aimed in one direction—at the rich. The millennium-old dam burst open and the roaring waters of the revolution rushed through the opening leaving death and destruction on its path. From this moment on, nothing in the world could stop this deadly rampage, even the provocateurs themselves were washed away.

The royalty, aristocracy, and clergy were the pride of Russian nation and culture. They were murdered first. They were those who used to build palaces, cathedrals and monuments for centuries; those who sponsored architecture, literature, art, music and science. Their wealth and properties were expropriated.

The next in line was Russian military establishment—the descendants of numerous generations of Russian officers; they were bred to defend and die for their country for centuries. Their properties were expropriated.

Then, the "bourgeois" class was eliminated—the most entrepreneurial, industrious part of the population who just started building industry and infrastructure in the backward country. Their properties were expropriated too.

Then, the class of "kulaks" was corralled and sent to Siberia to die; those were the most productive, hard-working peasants who fed not only Russia, but the European countries, as well. Their land and properties were expropriated.

The next was the class of the "intelligentsia" —the pride and brain of Russian culture. Writers and poets, artists and actors, musicians and composers, scientists and engineers followed the peasants or fled the country. The deadly irony is that they were those who promoted and supported the revolution.

In other words, the class envy was a powerful, but indiscriminant weapon of mass destruction in the hands of the socialists. It was an equal opportunity destroyer that eliminated one group of population after another non-stop, even those who promoted and supported it. When dust of this absurdity settled down, millions of people were gone.

Voltaire was right when he said: "As long as people believe in absurdities, they will commit atrocities."

If you think that the class envy is the most destructive weapon in the hands of socialists, you are wrong. A new even more powerful weapon is being built by socialists using the bankrupted script of the class envy. It may be called the "World Envy"—to make one group of nations envy another group.

In this scenario, the entire world is divided into two classes of nations: "the haves" and "the have-nots." The first group is the advanced and prosperous nations, mostly of the Western civilization; the second group is backward and poor nations of the world.

Now, the roaring envy energy and hate of billions is being combined, and the "we-are-the-world" crowd is channeling it toward the most ingenious, industrious, productive and thus prosperous part of the world population with a possible global destruction on an apocalyptic scale.

AFTERWORDS

One day, my 4-year old granddaughter Bella played a puzzle card-game following the rules. Suddenly, she changed the rules of the game set up by the game creator. But the picture obtained on the cards at the end of the game was a grotesque distortion of reality Bella used to enjoy around her. This fiasco convinced her to play by the rules again but probably not for long.

You can say that this is a familiar whim of a small child playing a game. But you can look at this trivial event at a different angle. Stunningly, but it is a microcosm of Man's behavior in his strained relationship with Nature. In fact, Nature gave Man a deck of cards to play a puzzle-game called Life and taught him to follow the rules. And Man has been playing this game with Nature by the rules ever since enjoying a beautiful picture at the end as a reward. (In fact, the capitalist free-market societies followed these rules as close as possible and brought unprecedented prosperity and freedom).

Then, the socialists have come and rebelled against Nature. They changed the rules to improve the capitalist game. They thought that the new picture on the cards at the end of the game would be more beautiful than reality. They expected to see equality and prosperity in that picture; altruism and freedom; and rejuvenated human nature. But what they got instead was just the opposite: hidden inequality and outrageous poverty; worst form of egoism and virtual slavery; abuse, perversion and degradation of a human nature. Man has finally come to senses and abandoned this fruitless and unnatural detour to socialism. Man returned to the old game and plays now by the rules of free-market capitalism as intended by Nature.

So, what is socialism? In fact, socialism is a product of an immature human mind; a mind of an infant on a scale of time and Life created by Nature. How much does an infant know about the game developed by Nature for millions of years? Can an infant predict the real consequences if the rules of the game are changed? Does an infant know how detrimental and dangerous those changes might be?

Man does not comprehend Nature's intentions. Socialist ideals of equality, altruism and rejuvenation of a human nature go against Nature. They come together as a package. Since *enforced equality* means taking from others, the pillage cannot be achieved without coerced "live-for-others" *altruism.* Since equality and altruism go against *human nature*, human nature has to be suppressed in order to be "rejuvenated."

In the eyes of Nature, the socialist ideals are absurdity. But it is not evident to most people until it is too late: until you end up living in a socialist country like the former USSR. This unnatural social structure started dying right at birth and passed away peacefully from *natural* causes relatively young, just at 70 years old.

Therefore, let's resort to an allegory for the last time to illustrate this point clearly. Let's imagine that community organizers, the proponents of socialist ideals are suing capitalism—the embodiment of inequality, self-interest and inborn vices of a human nature. They present a seemingly valid and convincing case in favor of the socialist ideals in the Circuit Court of...Nature.

All rise! Nature's Court is in session! Honorable Judge Nature is presiding. Socialist ideals vs. Reality!

"Your Honor! Over the years, the most brilliant human minds have been studying the Tree of Life created by Nature. When ignorant and uneducated people look at this tree, they see a rosy picture erroneously taken for reality. They see a beautiful tree growing in the sun and think that this is the perfect creation of Nature. The roots, stems, branches and leaves—all parts of the tree are viewed as one incredible, mind-boggling living organism. And because it exists for millions of years, they think that a "limited" human mind will never fully comprehend the complexity and perfection of this living organism; the intricate, mysterious and mutually beneficial relationships between its parts.

Nonsense! This picture is an optical illusion born by ignorance. We, intellectuals, do not trust our eyes; we look at this picture through scientific-socialist glasses; and what we see is a different tree, different relationships and different reality."

"Is there something wrong with the Tree?" Judge Nature asks pricking up her ears.

"Your Honor, with all due respect, we are concerned about wisdom of Nature that created this tree. Just look at the rich roots—they are filthy, crooked and ugly. They suck the nutrients out of the soil with insatiable greed, just for themselves. The rich roots do not pay their fair share. Although they trickle up some nutrients to the hard-working middle class stems and branches, and the starving, poor leaves, this is not enough.

We feel that Nature was wrong to create a tree with roots, and we want to correct this mistake of Nature. We want economic equality. We want to expropriate all nutrients illegally obtained by the rich roots and spread them among the poor leaves. Such redistribution will make the tree healthier. The roots should not be a part of a tree!"

"Are you sure that the poor leaves and the whole tree will be healthier without roots?" The Judge asks greatly surprised by such unprecedented request.

"Yes, we are sure, Your Honor! We have a socio-economic theory that predicts just that. Both the leaves and the tree will grow healthier without roots. This is because all the nutrients illegally obtained by a few rich roots will be shared equally by millions of poor leaves. There is no place for the rich roots in our socio-economic theory."

"But the opponents contend that the tree will get sick without roots; the roots are the only ones that possess unique skills to extract nutrients from the soil—the skills the leaves do not have. They predict shortages of nutrients and even famines," The Judge warns.

"Your Honor, the opponents use those excuses to preserve the status-quo and continue the exploitation of the starving poor leaves by the rich root-parasites!"

"Are you sure that those rich roots will agree to part with all they have?" Nature asks obviously confused by such unnatural logic of the plaintiff.

"Of course, your Honor! Our theory provides for means of expropriation. We have axes, scissors and spades, which will be instrumental in convincing the roots to cooperate voluntarily."

"But will the small amount of the expropriated nutrients be enough to feed those millions of leaves for a long time?" The Judge asks in astonishment.

"Of course, Your Honor! There will be no poverty on the planet Earth from now on and forever!

"Then, how, in the world, will those nutrients be shared among millions of leaves equally?" The Judge gasps in disbelief. She has never heard anything like that before.

"Your Honor, all the leaves will be reeducated and forced to live altruistically for others. They will be coerced to care about others more than about themselves. As for the fresh buds and leaflets, they will be brainwashed that all their possessions; labor and talents; thoughts, choices and wishes; body and even lives do not belong to them; they belong to others. This altruistic lifestyle will ensure equality among the leaves even if the nutrients are in short supply."

"But this is not possible! Every leave is born as an egoist and will act naturally in its self-interest. To share scarce resources equally means to go against leave's nature," The Judge sharply interrupts the plaintiff irritated by the absurdity of the proposal.

"Your Honor, our theory explains in details how to suppress the leave's nature and rejuvenate it. The leaves that refuse to share will be temporarily separated from the tree and concentrated in "rejuvenation" centers until we get rid of their egoism. As for the fresh buds and leaflets, they are born with a clean mind; it is our duty to fill them with the right values."

"...Well, well, well!" Judge Nature gasps with indignation. "Unbelievable! Let's take a recess for 15 minutes (on Nature's time—70 years on Man's calendar). When I return, I will make a thorough inspection. Be prepared to demonstrate how this unnatural scheme works. But I am warning you, if it does not, I will pull a plug on this fantasy of yours. Court is adjourned until the first inspection!" a giant hammer bangs on the table rumbling like the Big Bang.

So, did the community organizers cut off the roots of the tree in spite of Nature's warning? Of course, they did. In the name of Fairness and Equality, and on behalf of the poor, they uprooted the roots-parasites that were tirelessly and unnoticeably pumping up nutrients and moisture to the stems and leaves. They expropriated all the nutrients "illegally" obtained by the roots and redistributed them among the poor leaves. Their intentions were good—to eliminate poverty among the poor leaves and to make the tree healthier.

"O-o-ops! What has happened?" The community organizers are puzzled and confused. "We cannot understand why the tree gets sick and is dying without roots? Our theory predicts..."

Well, Man has a mind of a limited capacity. So do the social theories born in that mind. How outright arrogant is to think that Man can teach Nature how to grow a tree! Nature has millions of years of experience in her impressive resume!

The Russian socialists/communists killed millions of the most productive peasants as a "bourgeois class" because they did not fit their Marxist theory. Those peasants were the roots of the Russian society tree; they were nurtured by Nature for hundreds of years to live off the land. Those peasants fed not only Russia, but the Europe, as well. O-o-ops! The mutilated tree without roots has doomed more than 200 million leaves to wither. Without the peasants-roots, the Russian people were suffering from starvation and chronic food shortages for 70 years before Nature pulled a plug on that unnatural absurdity called socialism.

Now, new generations of socialists say that it was an honest mistake! The tree got sick and died not because the roots were cut, but because *those* community organizers were not that smart. But this is not all. Just listen to this! The most shameless and embarrassed socialists from academia say now that the socialism built in the USSR was not socialism at all; in fact, it was...*state capitalism*!!!

...Just...just...just give me a break! Are you, new builders of socialism, saying that those Russian Marxist-Leninist-Stalinist community organizers were stupid and did not have a clue what they were building for all those 70 years?

But what does it say about our domestic "builders" of socialism—progressives and community organizers; Marxists and leftists from mainstream media, Hollywood and academia? They enthusiastically supported and glamorized those stupid Marxist-Leninists; they were whole-heartedly embracing them; they still slobber from affection teaching Marxism at universities.

In other words, in the US, they were helping the stupid to bury capitalism and build socialism, while the stupid were building...capitalism in Russia...by mistake! What a bunch of stupid builders!

Now, new builders of socialism are asking for the second chance; they promise to do it right this time; they promise to build real socialism.

Man! Will you give those "builders" the 2ⁿᵈ chance?

Nature does not trust the qualification of the builders who offer to build a house called socialism, a better place to live. Like my 4-years old granddaughter, they also changed the rules of the game, the rules of construction and the Structural Code. Just look at their glorious design!

The foundation is built on a shaky, sandy ground of economic equality; the walls are erected from mud-and-straw bricks of "live-for-others" altruism; the bricks are loosely stacked together without mortar of competition and incentives. And look at the resumes of those ignorant "builders" themselves: they don't know how to build—they are experts in ...demolition! They have no clue about practical construction and technical disciplines; what they know well is the theories of class envy instead.

Would you allow such builders to build your house? Would you approve their design? For how long will such house stand before collapsing? Not for long because it will be demolished at the first inspection.

So, did Nature. Nature did not allow the socialists to do such outrageous violations of the Building Code of Life! Nature has demolished their house at the first inspection!

Man! Do you want to live in such house again?

Socialism is an undeveloped, foreign to Nature product of a limited human mind. Like the aids virus cannot live outside of a human body, socialism cannot live outside of a human mind—Nature kills it fast!

REFERENCES

Chapter 1: Wisdom: Nature vs. Man

1. Wikipedia, Ferrari.
    [Notes: Ferrari; length: 4.5 m (15 ft); weight: 1,350 kg (2,976 lb); maximum on-road speed: 298 km/hr or 83 m/sec (186 mph)].

2. Diseno-art.com. Platune-Sand-X bike.
    [Notes: Platune-Sand-X; maximum on-road speed: 186 km/hr or 52 m/sec (115 mph)].

3. Wikipedia, Cheetah.
    [Notes: Cheetah; length: 1.24 m (4.1 ft) average; weight: 44-kg (96 lb); maximum speed: 112 km/hr or 31 m/sec (70 mph)].

4. Wikipedia, Soviet Submarine K-222.
    [Notes: Project 661, Papa K-222 class nuclear submarine with titanium hall; length: 105 m (350 ft); maximum speed: 82.8 km/h or 23 m/sec (51 mph); speed relative to body length: 23 m/sec / 105 m = 0.22 body length/sec].

5. Wikipedia, Sailfish.
    [Notes: Sailfish; length: 3 m (10 ft); maximum speed: 112 km/hr or 31.1 m/sec (70mph); speed relative to body length: 31.1 m/sec / 3 m = 10.4 body length/sec].

6. Wikipedia, Space Shuttle.
    [Notes: US space shuttle; length: 56 m (184 ft); weight at liftoff: 2 million kg (4.5 mil lb); speed: 27,904 km/hr or 7,751 m/sec (17,440 mph); speed relative to body length: 7,751 m/sec / 56 m = 138].

7. Wikipedia, White-Throated Needletail.
    [Notes: White-Throated Needletail; length: 0.21 m (0.8 ft); weight: 93 g (0.2 lb); speed: 168 km/hr or 47 m/sec (105 mph); speed relative to body length: 47 m/sec / 0.21 m = 224].

8. Wikipedia, Rutan Voyager.
    [Notes: Experimental airplane Rutan Model 76 Voyager; built in 1986; flied without refueling 41,600 kilometers (26,000 miles); weight: 4,400 kg (9.690 lb) fully loaded; distance-to-weight efficiency: 41,600 km/4,400 kg = 9.45 km/kg].

9.　　Wikipedia, Arctic Tern.

[Notes: Arctic Tern, a migratory bird; length: 33-36 cm (13-15 in); weight: 86-127 g (0.19-0.28 lb); average weight: 106 g (0.23 lb); travels 22,000 kilometers (14,000 miles) from Farne Island, UK to Melbourne, Australia; distance-to-weight efficiency: 22,000 km / 0.106 kg = 207,500 km/kg].

10.　　Wikipedia, Apollo-Saturn V.

[Notes: Apollo-Saturn V flied 384,000 km (239,000 miles) to the Moon and back; weight fully loaded: 3 mil kg (1.36 mil lb); distance-to-weight efficiency: 768,000 km/3,000,000 kg = 0.256 km/kg].

11.　　Ayn Rand, The Virtue of Selfishness. The Objectivist Ethics. A Signet Book, p. 24.

Chapter 2: Nature vs. Equality

1.　　National Oceanic and Atmospheric Administration, National Climatic Data Center. Dec. 2009, Global Analysis Report. State of the Climate, Global Analysis, Global Temperatures.

2.　　US Census Bureau. Income, Poverty and Health Insurance Coverage in the US, 2008, Sept 2008.

3.　　Congressional Budget Office. Historical Effective Federal Tax Rates 1979-2005, Dec. 2007. Summary Table 1, Effective Tax Rates, 2004 and 2005. (http://www.cboftpdocks/88xx/doc8855/Effective TaxRates.shtml#1011537)

4.　　Average Earnings Worldwide. The Boston Globe, Oct 7, 2007.

5.　　World Bank, World Development Indicators Database 2009, revised 9 July, 2010. Gross National Income per capita, 2009.

6.　　Abraham Lincoln. Reply to New York Workingmen's Democratic Republican Association, March 21, 1864."

The Collected Works of Abraham Lincoln, ed. Roy B. Basler, vol. 7 (New Brunswick, N.J.: Rutgers University Press, 1990), 259-260.

Chapter 3: Nature vs. Altruism

1. Hamilton, W. D. 1964. The genetical evolution of social behavior, I, II. Journal of Theoretical Biology, issue 7, 1-52.
2. Trivers, R.L. 1971. The evolution of reciprocal altruism. Quarterly Review of Biology. 46: 35-57.
3. Academic Dictionary and Encyclopedias. St Thomas Aquinas in the "Summa Theologica", I:II Question 26, Article 4.
4. The Bible, Leviticus 19 and Matthew 22.
5. Stanford Encyclopedia of Philosophy, 5.3 Ethics and sociology, Comte.
6. Ayn Rand. The Virtue of Selfishness; Collectivized Ethics. A Signet Book, p. 93.
7. Martin Reuter, et al. Investigating the genetic basis of altruism: the role of the COMT Val158Met polymorphism. Oxford Journals, Social Cognitive and Affective Neuroscience. Published on line on October 28, 2010.
8. Randall, J. E. 1962. Fish service stations. Sea Frontiers, 8: 40-47.
9. Wilkinson, G. 1984. Reciprocal Food Sharing in the Vampire Bat. Nature, 308.
10. Cheney, D. L. & Seyfarth, R. M. 1990. How monkeys see the world: Inside the mind of another species. University of Chicago Press. ISBN 9780226102467.
11. Wikipedia, Altruism in animals.

Chapter 4: Nature vs. Nurture

1.   Richard Pipes. 2003. Communism, a History. A Modern Library Chronicles Book, The Modern Library, NY, p.7.
2.   Wikipedia, Tabula Rasa.
3.   Heldriss of Cornwell (c.1250-1300, 1992). Silence. Roche-Mahdi, Sarah (ed. and trans.). East Lansing, MI: Colleagues Press, Ltd.
4.   Philip Groff and Laura McRae. Nature-Nurture Debate in 13th Century France. Paper presented at the Annual Meeting of the American Psychological Association, Chicago, August 1998.
5.   John Locke. Essay Concerning Human Understanding. Kenneth P. Winkler (ed.), pp. 33–36, Hackett Publishing Company, Indianapolis, IN, 1996.
6.   Claude-Adrian Helvétius. *De l'esprit* or Essays on the Mind and its Several Faculties. English translation by William Mudford, 1807, Google Books.
7.   Galton, Francis. 1874. English Men of Science: Their Nature and Nurture, London, Macmillan and Co., p.12.
8.   B.F. Skinner. 1972. Beyond Freedom and Dignity. New York, Vintage Books.
9.   Edward O. Wilson. 1982. Sociobiology, The New Synthesis. The Belknap Press of Harvard University Press, Cambridge, Massachusetts, and London England, 7th Printing.
10.   Tomorrow's World. The Ten Commandments, by Roderick C. Meredith.
11.   Wikipedia, Homo Genus.
12.   A Hebrew-English Bible (according to the Masoretic Text and the JPS 1917 edition). Exodus, Chapter 20:12 and 20:13.

13.   Steven D. Levitt & Stephen J. Dubner. 2009.
      Freakonomics. HarperPerrenial, p. 21.

ACKNOWLEDGEMENTS

I want to thank my daughter Victoria Malin Gregory and my son Frank Gregory for their wise, valuable advice and encouragement in the process of writing this book.

A special thank-you I owe to my wife Mila Malin for her support and understanding throughout difficult times.

And most credits go to my precious, little grand-daughter Isabella Rand Gregory, a mystery of Life, who inspired me to write this book.